Antelope Bill

ANTELOPE BILL

By

Parker I. Peirce

Drawings by Mary Mitchell

Ross and Haines, Incorporated
Minneapolis 15, Minnesota - 1962

Table of Contents

Antelope Bill's First Trip Among the Sioux	8
Captivity of Mrs. Wakefield	49
An Insult	52
The-Man-Who-Closed-the-Gate	53
Incidents	71
Antelope Bill's First Buffalo Hunt	73
A Visit to Little Crow's Home	80
A Sick Man	81
The Brown Family	83
Sometings Go Buzz-Buzz	84
Minus One Ear	87
Horses Tails Made Use of Many Ways	91
The Killing of the Jewett Family Near Mankato	92
The Capture by the Sioux in 1862 of John Schurch a Lad of 15	94
Remarks Concerning the Savages of The Northwest	107
Battles of Birch Coolie and Wood Lake Reminiscences of the Indian War	115
Birch Coolie	132
Execution of 38 Sioux Indians at Mankato, Minn.	149
The Gallows	169
Order of Execution	169
An Incident	173
The Resurrection	173
Camp Mystery	174
Antelope Bill's Poem	183
Strike-The-Ree, a Once Famous Indian Lately Called to the Happy Hunting Grounds	187

Author's Note

The author of these pages was an eye-witness to about all of the events recorded here, and has endeavored to acquaint the reader with unvarnished facts connected with our history.

Not one line of fiction is recorded here and no attempt has been made to cover faults of expression. Frontier phrases have not been avoided.

The within written pages are from the journal of a boy of seventeen years who was saved from the tomahawk and scalping knife, by a friendly Indian. He most sincerely hopes that a degree of thankfulness will rise in the mind of the reader as he compares the perilous past with the peaceful present.

PARKER I. PEIRCE
Marshall, Lyon County, Minn.

Antelope Bill's First Trip Among the Sioux

From childhood days upon the sea-coast of Maine, till the removal of my father's family to Mankato, Minnesota, in the early fifties, I had earnestly wished to meet with an Indian.

In the spring of 1862 I was a beardless boy of seventeen years.

I was filled with unrest and that desire for adventure which most boys of that age experience. I told my father that I should like to go up the Minnesota river among the Indians and work for the government. Father gave his consent telling me that the Indian agent was about to visit the Sioux (Soo) agency and would be up the river in a few days on the steam propeller, "The Favorite," and on his coming he would arrange with him for me. As expected, the agent conferred with father.

At first he said he had what men he wanted, but upon reflection decided to take one more. In the meantime my older brother Henry had concluded to go with me.

His going pleased me. I was glad of his company.

In those days boat arrivals were infrequent, so we waited patiently and some days elapsed before the "Jeanette Roberts" loaded with supply of goods for the Indians rounded the bend of the river on her upward trip at the same time blowing her peculiar dull whistle. Our home was in the country but brother Henry and myself were in town. We went aboard the boat and saw the captain. It was eleven o'clock A.M. The boat would move up the river at three o'clock P.M. Cabin fare was $5 and steerage fare was $2. Our pocket book being thin we took passage at $2 steerage. We went home, packed goods, and at three o'clock P.M., were on the boat. This was May 22nd 1862.

Boat bell rang. Ropes were pulled in and we were off.

Away we went making slow progress, for although the river was high the boat was very heavily loaded. Here homesickness came creeping over me.

I wished I were at home; but to jump ashore and go home would shew a lack of grit and I decided to stick to the boat.

There was nothing on the river to attract the eye save low timber and floodwood until we had journeyed four days, when at about four o'clock P.M., we saw far ahead of us, moving objects. Sure enough they were men.

My heart fairly jumped for joy. We could once more look upon some "human face divine." Their number seemed to increase, the nearer they came. At last I heard the captain say he guessed the Indians were glad to get their annuities by the way they were coming to the landing.

In a short time the whistle blew and we were at the landing. We went ashore and were among the Sioux—the most warlike tribe in the west.

Was the picture once drawn in our youthful imagination truthful? No. Words fail to express our disgust on seeing those creatures before us. A half mile walk up the hill brought us to the top of the bluff and to the Government or Lower Agency.

Not far distant from here, during the first days of September, on the opposite side of the river, the battle of Birch Coolie was fought eighteen miles above Fort Ridgley.

Here at this Lower Agency was located a church, and schoolhouse, a stone warehouse, a blacksmith shop, a hotel with a boarding house where the employees were fed and lodged. We stopped at the hotel and on inquiry learned that the Government Agent had gone to the Upper Agency at Yellow Medicine, thirty miles farther up the river. We staid over night and resumed our journey the next morning. Going about half a mile we came to the trading post.

There were three stores. We called at one of these. Here were Indians exchanging furs for flour and sugar and squaws buying beads. On the counter there were four or five half-breeds partly asleep.

The proprietor was a white man. We expected he would be glad to see some of his own race, but no; he had lost his affinity for ties like these. He was living with a squaw to whom he had been married for years. Going on from here we shortly passed large brick dwellings upon improved farms. These houses were furnished with pianos and other civilized furniture. The Indians were lying about their houses while the nearly nude papooses were running about and the women were performing the farm work. We passed Little Crow's village and coming to the Redwood river, crossed it near its mouth. Going a short distance up a high hill we came upon a broad plateau on which stood a large house. Seeing at a glance that white people lived here, we called for a drink of water. Receiving a polite invitation from the lady of the house we walked in and rested on chairs offered to us. The lady inquired of us our business and we were inquisitive enough to ask what they were doing up in these wilds.

We learned that the inmates of the house were boarding the farm hands who were improving Indian farms. The overseer of the farm hands, Mr. Joe Reynolds, was the husband of the lady of the house. Here were two young ladies. I reflected. How lonely they must be. But the truth was they were government employees and were receiving a good salary. After resting we left this homelike place to walk 22 miles farther before reaching the Yellow Medicine Agency.

Homesick again.

Onward we tramped, and when we had gone about half the distance we came across some Indians.

We had our coats thrown across our shoulders. They jerked them from us, talking to us in Sioux, which we did not understand. They were going in an opposite direction from us and we naturally turned our heads to see what they meant, expecting every moment to receive a bullet from their guns. After a while they threw our coats to the ground and motioned for us to come for them. They knew we were scared at first sight. We considered this a close call and travelled on till we came to a higher rise of ground. Then we had a good view of the country for miles around.

(Near here was fought the battle of Wood Lake a few months later.)

In June, 1862, Prof. H. B. Wilson, professor of mathematics, in Hamline University, located at Red Wing, Minn., resigned his position to assist his country in her hour of need. He took command of Company F., 104 men, a large percentage of whom were students from Hamline—pupils of their captain. He joined the Sixth regiment of Minnesota volunteers infantry. Captain of Co. F. Sept. 22 the battle at Wood Lake was fought. Capt. Wilson's company charged amid a shower of balls, on the double quick through a ravine and put the Indians to route. Capt. Wilson was severely wounded.

The country west of us being very flat we could see the Upper Agency and the American flag waving above it. This sight was refreshing; our journey's end was near.

We came to the valley of the Yellow Medicine. The banks were skirted by low timber; it flowed on for a mile or so and discharged its waters into the Minnesota, forming very nearly two right angles at its mouth. We looked down into the valley. Here were the buildings of the traders. We passed by them, and taking the trail which wound up and about the bluff came up the steep hill and reached our long desired resting place. We were at the government buildings. We went to the largest of these and inquired for the agent. He was within.

The jolly, pleasant man received us and directed us to a white house forty rods away, telling us that the boss farmer lived there.

We went to Mr. Goodell, the superintendent farmer. He told us he would find something for us to do in the morning. He showed us our room and bed. This was to be our boarding place. In a few minutes the supper bell called us to the table, where a repast was enjoyed, which the writer has never seen excelled since that time. After supper I went to my room to rest.

I was homesick and among strangers. I thought could I but be landed back to civilization I should be willing to give up my most important garments, with boots and hat. I was tired; every bone in my body ached. There were four occupants in the room besides my brother and myself, and I was told that here teamsters hauling Indian supplies farther west, often found lodgings. Bed time came. We tumbled into bed regardless of the noise about us and were soon in happy dreamland.

It seemed but a short time before we heard the breakfast bell calling, arousing us from our sleep. Where are we?

I jumped from bed and dressed in a hurry; I was desirous to make a good impression as an early riser. We breakfasted, then called on Mr. Goodell and told him we were ready for business. He told my brother Henry he would give him eighteen dollars per month. He looked at me, a moment, as if in a study, and then said he did not need me, as he was fullhanded. I was "thunderstruck." I thought a moment, then said: "Mr. Goodell, I am all tired out. My feet are blistered. I would like to stop a few days—would work for my board." "All right," said he. "I have a garden to make. Have you ever worked at gardening?" I replied. "Yes, sir, I excel at that work." Said he: "Come with me." He took me out a little south of the house, to a piece of wild prairie. Said he, "here I want a bed of beets, here a bed of carrots, here a bed of onions and lettuce; this and that for other things." I thought to myself, "This is tough;" but I made him think it was all right, for I was

ANTELOPE BILL

determined to please him, cost what it might. He told me where the hoe, the shovel and the axe were. The axe was to be used in driving stakes.

Before sundown I had the beets and carrots sowed. O! How tired I was. At supper time, Mr. Goodell wished to know how I liked farming for he had not looked at my work during the day. I expressed satisfaction with work, only the sod was decidedly tough. Said he: "I guess it is; how long do you think it will take you to make the garden?" I replied, "about a week, if it does not storm." All the time I was wishing it would storm for about a week.

Here let me say for the information of those who are unacquainted with the sod of the uncultivated prairie. The sod for two inches downward is a compact mass of tough, interwoven roots, and these of all sizes, from that of fine spool cotton, to the thickness of half an inch in diameter.

The next morning was lovely. The breakfast o'er, Mr. Goodell said his wife would give me the seeds when I would be ready for them. Probably she had not told him how the work had progressed. He said he was going to Lacqui Parle and should be absent for several days.

Another day's work was before me. At dinner time I had made good progress. I was thirsty quite often and went to the house for drink. I chatted with the women at these times, bringing them fresh supplies of water, kept their wood box well supplied with fuel. I was homesick again. I wished Mr. Goodell to be at home so I could get excused and retire to Mankato. I did not express my thought, and after deliberating, decided to "stick." Oh, those tough, sod-covered bluffs! Why does not Mr. Goodell break the sod with his team? But then, what does he care as long as he has not to do the work with his own hands? Thus, I soliloquized. The next day found me at the same job. My poor hands blistered! And one of my boots about gone, worn out by bearing on the spade to force it through the sod. Night came. Mrs. Goodell came where I was at work and said, "Parker, that patch is large enough for the potatoes." The next day at ten o'clock, the garden was finished. Mrs. Goodell told me to come to the house and clean up the dooryard, and by night I had it looking tidy indeed. Mrs. Goodell gave me much praise, and telling me to sit and rest awhile, I complied with her request without a second invitation. It was very warm; I was fatigued, and soon I was nodding, when a voice near by startled me. "Are you ill?" It was Mr. Goodell speaking to me. I explained to him the condition of the garden and dooryard. It was all satisfactory to him. Together we visited the garden. I saw by the expression of his face that he was pleased with my success. Said he: "Parker, do you think you can wheel this pile of dirt out to the cistern tomorrow?" Before the next night the dirt was piled by the cistern and besides a dozen pails of water and many armfuls of wood had been carried to the house. That night I was homesick and thought I had worked long enough for my board. If I stayed much longer I should be without skin. I decided to start for home in the morning.

Morning came. We had an early breakfast as there were teamsters who wished to be away to arrive at a certain point before sundown. Mr. Goodell did not rise as early as usual, so I hung around and chatted with those about me till the sun was quite high. Mr. Goodell was not up. I wished to be on my way home; I was very nervous. At about 9:30 o'clock Mr. Goodell made his appearance. I kept out of his sight till after breakfast when I went to him and told him I thought I had worked long enough for my board and wished to go back home, as I was rested. He replied: "Oh, no. We cannot do without you. The women will wash to-day, and you can help them." After a moment's reflection I decided to remain.

I spent a very pleasant day pounding clothes, bringing water, keeping up the fires, and picking over beans and dried fruit for the coming meal. The day after this, with brother Henry and two others, I worked on the meadow planting potatoes. Prompted by the bet of a pair of moccasins by one of the men, when noon came I asked Mr. Goodell how much he was allowing me as wages. The reply came, "eighteen dollars per month." I was satisfied. About 40 rods east from the agent's house was the government warehouse built of brick and two stories high. In the rear were T. J. Galbraith's rooms. A little north was Dr. Wakefield's residence; northwest was the boss-carpenter's residence, a large two story brick building. East from our boarding house was Mr. Given's, the second agent's house, and also the house of Mr. Noah Sinks, the clerk.

Traders, four in number, were half a mile away down below the hill. A mile or so away the Yellow Medicine flowed into the Minnesota river. There was timber on both streams and some on the bluff north of the agency. The government buildings stood on a high bluff one side extending and spreading out upon the prairie westward.

After planting potatoes for a few days government cattle were driven to the agency and Mr. Goodell placed them in my care for herding. Among the cattle were half a dozen cows. I would drive them south across the Yellow Medicine river, and stay with them till about eleven o'clock, when leaving them, I would come home for dinner. I continued to do this for a week. After that I drove them to the pasture and returning home left them till three o'clock P.M., when I would go for them, driving them home at six o'clock. Mr. Goodell said the balance of the time I could pull weeds in the garden, or help about the house. As it was a dry season few weeds grew and I had more time to assist about the house. Mrs. Goodell was like a mother to me and Mary Hayes like a sister.

Here I had a fine opportunity to study Indian character, as the Indians were our constant visitors. No Sioux would kill a Sioux. No Chippewa would kill a Chippewa. No Winnebago would kill a Winnebago.

Very few murders were committed by Indians of those of the same tribe. The punishment for murder was this: To be tied hands and feet; the ponies of the condemned were brought before him and killed. He was then whipped, cut with flints, and pricked with sharp sticks. This was continued until the murderer was nearly dead, when he was turned over to the medicine man for treatment. It is said "the Indian talks as he thinks!" Does he? No: Most emphatically. They consider their Great Spirit, their Manitou, not as a good spirit, but as one possessed of all the evil attributes which we ascribe to the chief of devils. Is each created being like the God whom he worships? Then the Indian is known by his cruelty. Cruelty instead of mercy. They have no pen, ink or mail carriers. How, then, do they send messages from the Mississippi to the Missouri river? They have trails which run in all directions for miles. It is known that friends and relatives travel such and such trails. All along such trails there are knolls or ridges. Those are selected for post-offices. (They do not employ a postmaster.) Here is placed a large pile of rocks which at a distance looks like a man. It can be seen for miles. The message is left at this pile of rocks by taking small stones and placing them in such a way that the receiver can read it, he alone understanding the signs. Sometimes instead of stones, sticks are stuck in the ground. No one has a right to disturb those any more than one has to open and read a letter belonging to another party. By these they can inform whether one has gone east, west, or to such a timber, like or river. Each locality is in some way, designated.

When one is sick, he receives treatment at his tepee or is taken to the medicine man. He is given an herb infusion; then the medicine man will beat his drum around the sick man's head at the same time chanting his incantations.

They manufacture two kinds of arrows; one is for killing game, and the other for warfare. The one used for killing game can easily be removed from the wound. It is rounded at point. The other for warfare is made of hoop iron and is pointed sharp. They are made with a straight shoulder back of point. They cannot be pulled out but must, if removed, be pushed through the flesh in which they are embedded. Sometimes they are covered with gum and when they strike the blood the gum will melt. When trying to remove the arrow, the head will remain. Hawk's feathers in the hair denote the number of scalps taken.

A large number of dogs around an Indian camp signify war. In battle, the chief will be located on a high elevation of ground. They use a looking glass to signal the army to go forward. They will never kill a bear, a snake or a wolf. The wolf they believe to be the dog of the Great Spirit. They never allow a white man to tell them a second untruth. One who has once deceived them had better remain at a distance.

They believe in dreams, especially the dreams of old women. They often look for an enemy advised by dreams. An old woman unable to work had better be dead, they think. The women are the ones who weep; the men never shed a tear. Blood never scares a brave, and to be called a coward, means blood. The Indian women will never tan or dress a hide which has more than one bullet hole in it. Two or more holes would denote want of skill in the use of the rifle.

When their friends die, they wrap them in blankets and put them on a scaffold built of poles or in a tree to remain till the flesh dries. Sometimes these bodies will be taken down and buried but this is seldom done. The women will put meat at the foot of the trees or "staging," for a time. This is given at sunset. The dogs and wild beasts come and devour this, but they think the Indians come from their happy hunting grounds and eat it. The guns and equipments of the Indians are wrapped and buried with them, as they will want to hunt in their happy hunting grounds as they do here. Their names —such as Cut Nose, Grey Eagle and Red Cloud, are given them at birth. In the tepee or out of it, the first object not her own which the mother sees after the birth of her child, gives name to the child. The mother saw a red cloud in the west (the door of the tepee being open) she called her son "Red Cloud." Another, whose husband had killed an eagle, in like manner called her child Grey Eagle."

I was satisfied with my place. I had only to drive the cattle and milk two cows for eighteen dollars per month. I could go and come when I pleased; my going was quite often. Mr. Goodell told me to take any of the horses from the stable and use whenever I chose to do so. I was happy in this and could imagine myself the "boss farmer" and Mr. Goodell the hired man. Not much occurred from day to day to change the monotony—the hum-drum way of living.

An old squaw came daily to get the leavings from our breakfast and one day she slyly took a butcher-knife, although she denied it. Mrs. Goodell refused to give her any more food till the knife should be returned. At length the thief returned the knife saying another squaw stole it and she found it. She became very friendly with the women and told them all the Sioux were doing or saying. Had they known this, it would have been death to her. There seemed to be a mystery about, pervading the very atmosphere. We entertained an undefined dread of the unknown and the whisperings of the old squaw did not diminish our unrest.

One week before that eventful day Aug. 17th, 1862, my attention was drawn to some oat leaves that were growing in the cowyard back of the stable. On them was the letter "B" as plain as if made by printer's ink. I called to Mr. Givens. He silently studied the leaves for awhile and then with emphasis exclaimed: "B is for blood." Sure enough; within a week blood came.

Before this, whenever our nation was engaged in warfare, the Indian was sure to take an aggressive part. The white settlers on our frontier and we at the agency bore this in mind and whispered it. At the same time events were occurring near by us of which we at the agency were ignorant but of which we were soon informed. The Indians—the most savage people the earth has ever known—these wards of our nation were suffering from wrongs both real and imaginary—were starving. Our civil war was then trying men's souls.

Suddenly in early August, there came a general uprising of the savage upon the helpless, peaceful inhabitants of our borders, north, west, and south. We have not time or room here to relate the atrocities committed. Terror filled the hearts and palsied the hands of "brave men."

About this time Standing Buffalo would come to the agency for annuities. He would dress nicely in blanket, leggins, beaded moccasins, and with plenty of paint upon his face. I heard a young lady say "he is handsome enough to kiss." He was indeed, a fine looking Indian. Whenever he came I would take him to the milkhouse and give him all the milk he could drink. No other Indian relished milk.

At one time the agent had all the chiefs come down to hold council and get a good dinner. The dinner would bring them from any distance. The agent exclaimed: "We will first have dinner and talk afterwards." The table was set for about twenty guests. Rev. Williamson was at the table and said "grace" in the Sioux language. He first requesting them to bow the head. All complied with the request excepting one; in eating he was about five minutes ahead of the party, and he kept the place as leader, to the last. Soon the food was out of sight. Not infrequently a hundred Sioux families would come down for their annuities and camp near the agency, get their rations and return to their homes some sixty miles away. Some lived near by in nice houses of brick with a cultivated piece of land about their dwelling place. They were ruled by chiefs and came in bands. The chiefs would draw the rations, then the Indians would sit in a circle while the goods were equally divided. I will say here each farmer was entitled to a yoke of oxen, a cow, plow and seeds, fish hooks and line, needles, guns and powder—in short, every needed thing which a farmer usually has upon his farm. I have known them to live in their tepees and put their ponies in their brick dwellings. The women performed the drudgery—were their slaves. Standing one day by the warehouse I saw dust flying in the distance. I spoke to Charley Renville, (the interpreter) about it. He said he thought it to be Indians coming after rations. After a little they made their appearance "pell-mell." They were after a Chippewa Indian; an enemy. Deadly hatred existed between the Sioux and Chippewa tribes. I saw a poor Chippewa inhumanly treated one day. His tortures were too cruel to relate.

The Indians were to receive from the government twenty dollars per head for each individual, children and all.

The last of July or the 1st of August, 1862, the Indians were to receive their pay. Generally on these pay days there would be trouble, as the Indians sometimes became unmanageable; so much so, that the agent concluded to send down to Fort Ridgley for Capt. Marsh (who was shortly afterward killed by the Indians) and his company. The captain could not come, so ordered his brave and fearless lieutenant, T. J. Sheehan with his company to the agency. They arrived and the money was looked for every day. The Indians would come and go. The agent told them to go home and attend to their corn and he would let them know when ready for them. Eight hundred of them came and camped half a mile above the agency. The agent asked them what they meant. They said they were afraid of the Chippewas and felt safer where the soldiers were. These one hundred soldiers were encamped opposite the warehouse in a circle. They had three Howitzers. Sometimes a party of the boys in blue would be out on a hunting or a fishing expedition. One morning I was out milking. Dr. Wakefield was near me doing the same. I inquired: "What is that shooting?" He replied "it is the Indians. They have sent the agent and Lieut. Sheehan word that they are coming down to salute them and not to be alarmed as they would do them no harm." I started milkpail in hand for the house. As I passed the corner of the warehouse I could see them coming. Their ponies were on the jump. Going on a few rods farther, I looked up. They had the soldiers surrounded, their guns cocked, and leveled on every soldier. I looked to the right and saw them shooting. They were seeing how near they could come to Mr. Sink's feet without hitting him. Soon they aimed at me. They shot a hole through my milk-pail and the milk streamed out. They made the dust fly at my feet with bullets; the ground was fairly black with Indians. One stood over me with a tomahawk raised telling me that if I stirred he would bury it in my skull. He could speak good English; we knew him by the name Josh. The soldiers were still surrounded. The Indians tried to remove the shells from the Howitzers. I saw an Indian rush over to Dr. Wakefield's and get an axe. An Indian was chopping at the warehouse door with a tomahawk, but making slow progress, till the axe from Dr. Wakefield's was brought, when the door soon came down. The agent told them they had lied to him. He said:

"You have the thing your own way. You may kill me and my family, but I will not consent to your taking the goods from the warehouse." The old chief replied: "They are ours and we are going to have them." One Indian drew up his gun and fired cutting the rope which held the flag. It came down. The agent told them, if they would disperse he would issue rations to them. He told them to come in the afternoon unarmed. They went back to camp taking only food enough for their dinner. One movement on our side and every person would have been killed. Such were their intentions. They had put out men, so that if one attempted to escape he would be shot. As soon as he had left the agent got the employees together and armed them. The soldiers moved camp to the warehouse. The Indians came down as ordered. The annuities were carried a short distance from the warehouse. The chiefs took, divided, and all went back to camp. Come to find out that morning these "reds" had shot one of our cows full of arrows. The agent thought the troubles were now passed and ordered the soldiers back to Fort Ridgley.

The money to pay to the Indians would not come for sometime. During the early days of August the agent organized the Renville Rangers taking all the employees at both the Lower and the Upper Agencies and about all the half-breeds. I was the only one left at the agency, excepting a few employees, Germans at the brickyards and those who had the care of the Agency. It was rather lonesome now. Occasionally a few Indians would come and hold counsel with the assistant.

At one time they brought a buffalo calf and presented it to the agent. At night, on bringing home the cows, I took one of the smallest and tied her in a corner of the fence and brought the young stranger to be adopted. She saluted it at first with her horns, and then with her heels. The calf paid no attention to this, but rather seemed to enjoy the sport. The cow finally subsided, adopted the calf, and became fond of it; in a few days it went to the pasture with her and the other cattle. It grew very fat and promising.

August 17th, I went to look after my cattle. Sure enough they were gone! I searched for them, riding very, very fast to get over as much ground as possible. I hunted high and low but at last gave up the search. It now became dark. I could not see. I rode past Kennedy's store. He was on the outside. Said he: "They are very much excited on the hill, are they not?" I replied, "I have been absent some hours; I know of nothing unusual." He informed me news had been brought that the Indian chief Little Crow, had killed a family on Beaver Creek. I put spurs to my horse and was soon at home. I met Mr. Goodell; he told me to put up my horse and hurry up and eat my supper as the Indians had broken out at the Lower Agency. I could not eat. Mrs. Goodell and Mary Hayes went up to the warehouse; the people at the agency had gathered there. Soon John Other Day and wife came, telling us the Indians were holding council near by. They wanted him to join them as they were going to kill all the whites. He had told them he would see them again. He kept his eye "peeled" for fear they would shoot him. He was all excitement. After awhile he wished me to go with him down towards the traders. So we each put on a blanket and took the trail, I keeping a little back of him. He met an Indian who told him they were going to kill all the whites. The Indian wished to know who I was. Other Day replied "a friend." He came to me and said "make for the warehouse as soon as possible." I obeyed his orders promptly; I knocked at the door. It was opened, and I went in. I may as well mention here events transpiring down over the bluff at the traders. When the Indians attacked the traders at Yellow Medicine, Pete Patrolle was outside in the brush expecting an attack; they thinking it was only a scare, as reports and scares were common. They were mistaken this time. Pete watched the Indian movements and saw they were in earnest.

ANTELOPE BILL

He left hastily on foot and followed the river for about seven miles. He found an opening and crossed over to timber. He had just entered it when on looking back he saw to "Bucks" (Indians) after him, while at the same time they fired their guns, shooting him through the body. He ran as fast as circumstances would permit down the bluff to the river, jumped in and made down the stream keeping under the bank with his head out of water. He heard his pursuers pass him several times, but as it was getting late in the evening, they abandoned the search. After dark he went up on the prairie, found a deserted house and slept on the floor until morning. He then started on his journey. Going a short distance, he espied an Indian camp near by. He turned back to the house and climbed overhead in the porch. In a short time a squaw came in and seeing blood on the floor which had dropped from his wound, looked up and saw him, exclaiming: "I will go and call my man and he will kill you." Pete begged of her not to tell him but it was of no use. She started away. Pete got down from the porch and made for the timber, but being weak from loss of blood was very slow in getting there. He followed the river hoping to reach the fort. In about three days he was picked up by soldiers, cared for, recovered from his wound and at length enlisted in the 1st Minnesota cavalry. He afterward saw some hard fighting and came out satisfied with victories gained.

I will now take the reader to the warehouse where I had taken refuge. There were four new arrivals; Charles Crawford, (the interpreter) a half-breed and two Indians. Charley said he would stick to us as long as there was a drop of blood in his veins. "So will the other Indians," he said. Soon John Other Day came to the door all out of breath, telling us that the Indians covered the prairies; had killed all the whites at the Lower Agency and were coming to get us.

He said the Traders discredited the reports with the exception of Mr. Kennedy, who had left for Fort Ridgley. We talked the matter over, and decided that if die we must we would sell our lives at a premium. The party consisted of twenty men and forty-two women. Major Galbraith, wife, and three children; Nelson Givens, wife, wife's mother and three children; Noah Sinks, wife and two children; Henry Eschelle, wife and five children; Mr. German and wife; Frederic Patrol, wife and two children; Mrs. Jane H. March, Misses Mary and Lizzie Sawyer, with their brother Charles Sawyer; Miss Mary Daly, Mrs. Eleanor Warner, Mrs. John Other Day and child; Mrs. Hamharn, N. A. Miller, Edward Cromsie, T.

Hawkins, Oscar Canfil, Mr. Hill (an artist, from St. Paul); J. D. Boardman, Parker I. Pierce, Dr. J. L. Wakefield, and several others. Occasionally some of our party would go slyly out and return to report that the Indians were holding council.

We had bales of blankets at the windows, and at the head of the stairs were barrels and loads of stone; on the arrival of the Indians these could be rolled down upon their heads. The women were armed with knives and axes and appeared brave. John Other Day reported that "the corn back of the house is filled with Indians." We decided not to fire the first shot, but were pounding out bullets, getting ready for an attack.

Charles Crawford and Indians were down stairs most of the time and seemed to be quite by themselves. We had given them our best rifles, leaving us with shot guns only. The night was dark and dreary. Those about us wore long faces. Dr. Wakefield was worrying about his wife and son who had started to go east by team with Mr. Gleason, and the husband was thinking they must have been at the Lower Agency or near there, when the attack commenced.

Mrs. Wakefield was taken captive and carried up the river where she was afterwards released by Gen. Sibley at Camp Release. She afterwards published a book in which she gave a pen picture of her journeying with the Indians. She describes them as they are riding in their stolen covered carriages; some dressed in the bridal costumes of those whom they had murdered. Black or dusky faces under cover of white satin bonnets! Every wheel that could be utilized was moving; even two wheels on which were poles, dragging one end on ground were loaded with Indians riding for pleasure.

Mrs. Galbraith was anxious for her absent husband and all of us were feeling that death might be near to each one of us. It was now all so still within doors. Not a sound of the wind was to be heard. It was threatening rain without. We were at the windows watching for the enemy to fire our buildings by putting combustibles on their arrows and shooting into the roof of the building. Bang! bang!!! went the guns down at the traders. At the same time a yelling like that of demons reached our ears. The war-whoop was sounding! We could see the flash of the guns, then all would be silent a few minutes. They started a fire by the buildings. It appeared as though they were having a feast. Someone went down stairs and behold! The doors were wide open. Those two Sioux d--s had deserted us. What were we to do! They knew how defenseless we were. The shooting we had heard was the signal for them to go. We discussed the matter. Said John Other Day: "If we start now, we shall all be killed." We heard a pounding at the door, and a familiar voice, saying, "For God's sake, let me in; I am shot!" We opened the door. Here was Mr. Garvie. (We called to mind the sentence: "B" is for blood.) As he stepped within doors he fell fainting. Reviving, he told us his story. He was standing in the doorway when a bullet fired from an Indian rifle hit him in the abdomen. The Indians were so earnest in stealing goods that they stepped over him unnoticed thus giving him an opportunity to crawl away to the bushes. Creeping as best he could, he had at length reached us. We hoped the Indians only intended to kill the traders but we concluded to start by the coming of daylight and if possible, make our escape. Some were for going immediately. John Other Day's advice was accepted. He said, "stay till daylight; if all is well, then start. If then you are compelled to fight, fight to the last. The Indians will show no mercy.

The firing without greeted our ears and then we pounded more for bullets as we had no moulds. Oh! how I wished for wings that we might fly away. This all seemed to me to be a dream. God's hand was leading us and we knew it not.

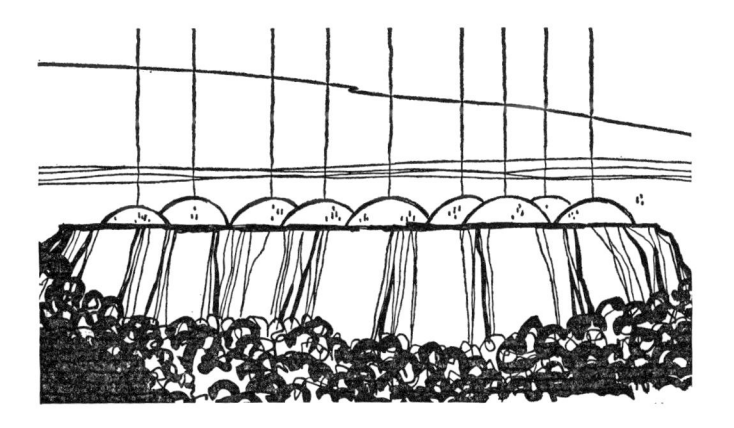

The gray dawn of the morning came. Mr. Goodell said, "there are no Indians about the premises. I think we shall find them in ambush when we start." He put some watchers on guard while the teams were being made ready for the journey. There were three men, foreigners, with us who stood at the door trembling like aspen leaves. Excepting these, all worked rapidly, as Mr. Goodell directed. I was stationed back of the stable at the top of the bluff. The sun began to lighten the heavens in the east. I heard the brush crackle and told Mr. Goodell Indians were coming. He said, "do not fire first." He, coming nearer, I motioned him to remain where he was. Soon an Indian made his appearance. I levelled my gun at him and inquired of him what he wanted. He said he wished to see Mr. Goodell. I told him to come along. I took my gun from my shoulder but watched him closely. He came and talked, telling Mr. Goodell he was sorry he could not go with us. (This was the old Indian, Renville, father of our deserter, Charley Renville).

All this time Other Day was scouting around. The teams were made ready, and the families loaded in. We took with us our wounded man Mr. Garvie. Going northeast passing Labelle's farm crossing the Minnesota river, it not being very high, we had no trouble in fording. I had one pocket loaded with bullets the other with powder. My powder in the lower edge of my pocket got wet. Finding a canoe, I took in Mr. Hill with others and crossed over, after which we hurried on and soon overtook the teams which were moving slowly. Mr. Garvie's wound was now very painful. On ascending, the summit of a high hill, I turned about to take a farewell look of the agency. Horrors! It was all ablaze. The black smoke was rising in clouds and circling above. Tears came to some eyes. We hastened on as fast as circumstances would permit. Two of our party going down to Joe Brown's farm on entering the house found our deserter, only "Charley Renville," who had nothing on his body for covering excepting his loin cloth, but had his gun; he said his horses were so poor in flesh they were unable to travel. He would not go with us. He said the Browns had gone to Fort Ridgley. The rascal! The deserter! A few miles further on a Frenchman joined our party. At a distance before us we saw what appeared to be men. By closer observation it appeared they were shaking their blankets at us. They were in the direction we wished to go. Some said, "they are Indians." Others said, "they are white men." We halted and prepared to fight. Other Day and the Frenchman went ahead but soon returned, saying the strange objects we had seen shaking their blankets at us were sand-hill cranes flapping their wings, and we felt safe once more. Clouds suddenly gathered in the west and soon the rain began to pour down in torrents; every circumstance now seemed to favor us.

Here, some of the party suggested leaving and going to Fort Ridgley. Other Day remonstrated, saying: "I do not wish to see you killed. I do not wish to be killed myself. I do not wish my wife killed." (She was a white lady whom he had married in Washington). "I am going across the country, although I have not been this way since I was a boy." With the exception of two Germans, all of us decided to go with Other Day.

Towards night, wishing to camp, we sent two men ahead to find a desirable place. They came to a house occupied by two Swede men, who were evidently in fear of the Indians. They could not speak English and seemed nearly wild with fright. Our party came to the house to spend the night. We gave the women and children bread and the men went without tasting food. All were glad to retire early. We put out our sentinels—two guards, placed one in a wagon, the other in a cluster of bushes. Those in the house placed their guns in a corner and went to rest as best they could. I laid down upon a board but found little rest, as these two Swedes kept us awake with their songs and devotional exercises; we could not quiet them. After a time they left us not knowing whither they went and we never saw them again. Going out to our guards, we found them fast asleep. On their awakening they assured us there was no danger to be feared till morning light. We, thinking otherwise, changed guards. We laid ourselves down again for a quiet sleep, when some one accidentally knocked down a gun, the charge passing through the clothing of one of the ladies. Had the Indians attacked us?—was the question. For a time all was excitement.

After quiet was restored down came a wooden bowl from overhead and struck me in the face. Thinking or dreaming of Indians I placed the bowl overhead again, but not far enough. Soon it came down again on my poor face. I put it this time upon the floor and slept quietly and soundly until morning. We awakened early the following morning. The women and children eating their bread we started. The men complained of being lame; I was lame, and then my poor face! We were off just as the sun was making its appearance.

August 19th we kept a northeasterly course and came to a settlement which had been abandoned. Some fowls remained but the cattle had been driven off. Not a crumb of food was to be found in the houses; only a few turnips and potatoes were to be found. Time was so precious it would not do to stop long enough to cook them. I felt like resting; my moccasins were worn out and my summer pants worn and ravelled to the knees worn by tramping through the tough prairie grass. We halted; the dust was rolling up in front of us and we perceived objects moving. Are these men on horseback before us? Mr. Goodell said "They are Indians, and are coming nearer; some are on ponies and some in wagons." We concluded to send a man on horseback to meet them. He went out a short distance and halted. Some men from the approaching party came up to him. "See these are white men." Mr. Sinks is coming back with them. Sure enough; it is Capt. Dodd on his way to reinforce New Ulm.

Here we are first informed of the atrocities committed at that place. Said Capt. Dodd: "If any of you wish to go with me jump in." Other Day and a few others with myself joined the party—"jumping in." Mr. Goodell remonstrated saying, "Parker, you have seen enough already and you may be very much needed by us." So I climbed out of the wagon to foot it once more. The country we passed over was a sad sight to look upon. Harvesting left in all stages; shocks unfinished and everything going to waste. At five o'clock we thought it about time to camp. We looked and saw a house before us and two horses tied in front. If Indians are here there are only two and we can easily meet them. We hurried on till within forty rods of them, when they, seeing us, came out of the house, mounted their horses and were away. We saw they were white men. We shouted to them, the women waived their shawls, and Dr. Wakefield shook a blanket. The more we shouted the faster they rode. We decided not to camp but to follow those men. After travelling two miles we saw a lake not far ahead of us and went directly toward it. Shortly we saw a body of men on horseback coming directly towards us.

We kept moving on and they coming nearer. At last we halted and sent a man ahead. They levelled their guns at him and held him there until they found out who he was. Being informed, they came up to us, and there was rejoicing. The two scouts sent out by them reported us as Indians. Cedar City is a town now located near this lake. There was a great uproar among the women and children. We told our story over and over again as requested till we were nearly hoarse. About sundown preparations were made for supper. Dr. Wakefield ordered porridge for us. It will not do to eat such hearty food as they are preparing for you." I did not follow his suggestions and consequently experienced extreme suffering in a few hours.

We were in a hastily constructed building, its dimensions being 60x60 roughly boarded. I retired early, taking my lodging under a wagon. At midnight the rain came down in torrents. My wagon box was like a fine sieve. I rose in the dark and crawled into the building between two men, my feet hanging out in the rain. These men were unconscious of my presence till informed in the morning. I ache, now, on calling to mind the fatigue which I experienced at that time. It was with difficulty that the fires were started this morning as nearly everything was so wet. At about nine o'clock the sun came out hot and dried the camp. Mr. Garvie was taken a short distance to a farmhouse where he was cared for, two of our men going with him.

We talked of our departure. Some decided to go to St. Paul, some to Shakopee and some to other points in the state. I was offered shoes and pants but did not accept them for reasons not here expressed. Mr. Goodell asked me to drive his team to Henderson, taking with me Mrs. Other Day and boy. I would say here that this little child was a full blooded Indian boy. A waif was found at the door. One night a cry was heard without. The door was opened, and a bundle found on the doorsteps. On looking within a baby was there and Mr. and Mrs. Other Day became foster-parents by adopting it. Doing as requested I was soon away over the prairie feeling secure from danger. Mrs. Other Day was communicative and told me of a grave mistake which her husband once had made by killing a negro, supposing he was taking the life of an enemy—a Chippewa. In the afternoon we arrived at Henderson and driving to a hotel I assisted Mrs. Other Day and son to alight. Here a crowd came together. The questions were heard on every side: "Where did that Indian come from?" "What are they here for?" "Where are they going?" "Rough looking," said another. We went into the sitting room. Sure enough the crowd followed. I heard one say, "let's kill that Indian." I thought it time to explain and did so. Their tune was changed immediately. Their hearts evidently were touched. Someone told an old Lady near by that there was an Indian at the hotel. She came down determined to kill him. Such was the excitement that it was better to keep him out of sight. A gentleman brought me a sum of money and taking me to a clothing store I was soon dressed in a splendid suit of clothes. We went to the stage office to buy a ticket to Mankato. They knew me and would not take a cent. News here reached me of Mr. Garvie's death. I retired early to avoid talking. After breakfast next morning I left Mrs. Other Day at the hotel and saying goodbye, I mounted the coach for St. Peter and Mankato. The Indians were reported as being near town and murdering the whites. All was terror. The stage agent told the driver he need not go unless he chose. Rumors of danger were afloat but the driver of the stage, Chris, decided to go on his way and "make the trip." The country along the way was deserted. When we arrived within half a mile of Mankato we found sentinels on guard and when we arrived at the postoffice hundreds had gathered to hear the news from below. I spoke to my old friends; they hardly recognized me, supposing I had been murdered. And then, such rejoicing as there was at my coming home. I met my father on the street, and he said: "You showed me the place where you would hide, should there be danger." You told me of this place; (when I was at the agency.) "I told mother I did not believe you were killed."

Captivity of Mrs. Wakefield

On the morning of Aug. 16th at the Upper Agency Dr. J. L. Wakefield felt very uneasy about his family, fearing the Sioux would rise and put on their war paint as all indications pointed that way. As George Gleason was going to St. Paul, Dr. Wakefield advised his wife to go with him and from there, go East, on a visit. After some hesitation she consented and packed her trunk with a few necessities. The writer (?) hitched up the team and all got in. On the back seat was Mrs. Wakefield carrying her babe in her arms and with her little boy beside her while

Mr. Gleason occupied the front seat. All being ready, with a pitiful goodbye, they took their departure. Mrs. Wakefield told the writer she had a presentment of danger after they started. Taking the Lower Agency road they had gone but a short distance when they met an Indian, who, as they passed him, told them to go back. Mrs. Wakefield to Mr. Gleason, "what does that mean." His reply was "oh pshaw! that is nothing. He only wants to say something," as they drove on leisurely. Mrs. Wakefield often implored Mr. Gleason to turn back but he would laugh and assure her there was no danger. When they arrived opposite Joe Brown's place, she said, "come Mr. Gleason, we had better go over the river to Mr. Brown's;" but he only smiled and put her off once more. Thus they travelled on till within two miles of the Agency when Mrs. Wakefield discovered smoke as though the whole country was afire. Shortly afterward they saw two Sioux a short distance ahead coming towards them. These Indians passed them but as soon as they were by turned and fired, the bullet passing over the boy's head and striking Mr. Gleason. He fell out of the wagon and the horses started to run, but one of the Indians caught them. Mr. Gleason lay where he fell, mortally wounded. His last words to Mrs. Wakefield were: "Why did I not hear to you." Then the Indians shot him again killing him

ANTELOPE BILL

instantly. One of the Indians was going to kill Mrs. Wakefield, but protested, saying, "she is the doctor's wife and he has befriended us." "No the other said she is the agent's wife." The first Indian was convinced and her life and that of her boy was spared. One of the Indians jumped into the wagon and drove to camp. During their drive thither Mrs. Wakefield threw out wraps and other things so that the whites might follow and know where she was. At the camp she found other white captives. Soon a squaw came around with a dress for her to put on in place of the one she wore. She immediately recognized this dress as one she had helped a friend make a few week's previous. She saw one of the squaws wearing one of her best black silk dresses as she did the cooking, the skirt dragging through the ashes as she walked back and forth. The Indian children had gold watches and other valuable jewelry to play with and the Indians were wearing the wheels out of gold watches in their ears. Among the captives was a German woman who was continually lamenting the loss of her house and stock, though she seemed to show no anxiety about the rest of her family, nor did her present situation seem to worry her in the least. Mrs. Wakefield did not see her little boy for two days and of course was greatly worried about him. A Miss Brown, one of the captives, told her he was at another camp nearby and that she would bring him to her; she did so, but he hesitated to come as he was having a good time riding the ponies and shooting with bow and arrows and when he arrived he was togged out in Indian costume and paint so that his mother hardly knew him. Mrs. Wakefield and children were released in the fall of 1862.

An Insult

The writer's brother was at the Upper Agency, Yellow Medicine, a week before the Indian massacre. He was warned to leave that country by a friend as the Indians were becoming unmanageable, manifesting disturbance in several ways. He provided himself with food and hastened across the river to the main road intending to go to New Ulm and thence to Mankato. Arriving at the top of the bluff he met two Indians who hailed him with How-How, and dismounted their ponies. Seizing him, they took the food and what little change he had; then spit tobacco juice in his face which was not very pleasant but nevertheless he had to take it. They then told him to go without a second warning, thinking he could endure such torments as that if he could get out of the country safely. His friend was right for he left the next day. That friend was my father. He also arrived at Mankato without any interruption. There was great anxiety in his mind as he had two more sons in the Indian country; one in Renville Rangers and the other perhaps in his hiding place—River Bottom, which he had picked out weeks before.

THE-MAN-WHO-CLOSED-THE-GATE

The Thrilling Story of the Brave and Fearless Defenders of Fort Ridgely, During Little Crow's Revolt and Massacre of 1862.

For thirty six years in all the tribes of the Sioux, "Man-Who-Closed-the-Gate" has been a name to conjure with. Capt. Timothy J. Sheehan is the name he bears among the pale-faces; and his home is in St. Paul. In his old age he is serving in the United States as a deputy marshal. The gate he closed was the entrance to the lower Minnesota valley; it was Fort Ridgely. Five days he and his little command held that frontier post while the hosts of painted warriors surged over the surrounded prairies and dashed against its defenses in vain. They were five precious days.—They gave time for the eastern part of the valley to arm and take the offensive. Repelled at New Ulm, and hurled back at Ridgely, Little Crow saw the beginning of the end before Sibley appeared on the upper waters of the Minnesota and administered the defeat of Wood Lake.

At the breaking out of the war of the rebellion Capt. Sheehan enlisted as lieutenant in Company C., Fifth Minnesota. At first they were stationed at Fort Ripley, where Capt. Francis Hall was commandant. On June 19th, 1861, pursuant to orders, Lieut. Sheehan with fifty men marched to Fort Ridgely, a distance of 200 miles and arrived there on the 28th. Two days after arriving at the fort the command was ordered to report to Maj. Thomas Galbraith at the Sioux agency on Yellow Medicine river. With a 12 lb. howitzer, Sheehan arrived with Lieut. Gere at Upper Sioux Agency July 2nd. The Indians were anxiously awaiting the distribution of supplies and annuities and were very restive. They addressed the lieutenants thus "We are braves. We have sold our lands to the great father. The traders are allowed to sit at the pay table and take all our money. We wish you to keep the traders away from the pay table, and we desire you to make us a present of a beef." A conciliatory but not satisfactory reply was made to this request. The Indians were hungry. Dances and other demonstrations became quite common. The number of the savages continued to increase, and dissatisfaction was felt and increased because of the non-arrival of the annuities. On July 18th the Indians declared they were starving. To placate the Indians, Maj. Galbraith assured them he would soon count them, issue provisions and send them to their homes to await the arrival of the delayed annuities. The counting was accomplished without trouble but on Aug. 4th matters had now changed and the Indians were hungry and restless. Lieut. Sheehan returned to Yellow Medicine after an unsuccessful hunt for Inkpaduta and his band of horse thieves. The Indians sent word that they desired to make a peaceful demonstration. No remonstrance was offered, and the little detachment was soon surrounded by 800 Indians some mounted and some on foot. They circled round and round the troops, firing their guns in the air shouting, dancing and contortioning. Suddenly the leader of the party struck his hatchet into the door of the government warehouse. The situation now became serious. The Indians began to cock and prime their guns standing not over a hundred feet from the troops. Had there been one hothead in the command, had a single man discharged his rifle, every one of them would have been murdered on the spot. The Indians were ripe for the deeds of deviltry they performed two weeks later. They wanted supplies and proposed to take them by force while intimidating the troops. Bloodshed was not the primary object. They had already begun to carry flour out of the warehouse. Lieut. Gere acted promptly. The single mountain howitzer he had, was trained on the warehouse door. Instantly the red warriors fell back from line of aim, leaving a lane, through which Lieut. Sheehan, Sergeant Trescott and sixteen men marched straight to the government building, never trembling or swerving an inch. Sergeant Trescott drove the Indians out of the warehouse while Lieut. Sheehan conferred with Major Galbraith. A number of councils and conferences resulted in an amicable settlement of the trouble, and all danger of an outbreak seemed to have been averted. Lieut. Sheehan and his men returned to Fort Ridgely, and on August 17th set out on the return march to Ft. Ripley. On the evening of the 18th his command was encamped at a point between New Auburn and Glencoe, forty-two miles from the fort. Suddenly, into the camp rode Corporal McLean straight from the fort with orders from Capt. Marsh to return at once. When that order was received, poor Marsh and most of his reconnoisance company and the whites at the upper and lower agencies had been murdered. Lieut. Sheehan lost no time; that night his soldiers marched 42 miles in nine hours and fifty minutes, such a march as was never equalled by infantry.

At 9 o'clock a.m., they reached the fort to which refugees from all the country around were flocking.

That same morning the Indians held a great council on the prairie about two miles from the fort and were addressed by Little Crow himself. It had been his plan to attack Fort Ridgley at once, but the council determined to attack New Ulm first. The Indians were then observed to pass to the southward on the west side of the river. The next morning the little garrison of the fort was further strengthened by the arrival of a company of fifty recruits under Lieut. Gorman, the company having been hastily organized at St. Peter, and courageously marched all night with but three rounds of ammunition for their antiquated muskets. On the 18th Clerk Wyckoff had arrived with $70,000 in gold for annuities. The total fighting strength of the force, including armed civilians, was now augmented to 180 resolute men while the non-combatant men, women and children in the fort, numbered 300.

Lieut. Sheehan, by virtue of seniority of rank, took command of the fort immediately upon his arrival, and forthwith set about active preparations for the battle which was sure to come. The men of Company B of the Fifth regiment being expert in the use of artillery, were assigned to the management of that in the fort of which three pieces were put in service at once. Ordinance-Sergeant Jones was put in charge of a six-pounder field-piece, and Sergeant James

G. McGrew and J. C. Whipple, an experienced artillerist, were each assigned command of a twelve-pounder mountain howitzer.

The fort itself, was a fort only in name. Like all of our forts on the frontier it was designed more as a military cantonment than as a place where defense could be made. It has not been the policy of our troops in the Indian wars to await attack. The fort consisted of a group of buildings surrounding an open square ninety yards across. It stood on a spur of high prairie land about a half mile northwest from the river. Along the north and east side of the spur on which the fort stood, a deep ravine extended southeasterly into the valley. The edge of the bluffs of the river valley lay about 300 yards from the south side of the fort, while from a point nearly opposite the southwest angle of the fort another lateral ravine penetrated the spur to within 300 feet of the corner. All of the buildings were of frame or log construction excepting the two-story stone barracks buildings on the north end of the quadrangle.

Repulsed at New Ulm, Little Crow turned back up the valley and made his dispositions for the siege of the fort. At one o'clock in the afternoon of August 20th, Little Crow himself appeared on horseback just outside of range of the pickets, and seemed to desire a conference. But the pickets on the northeast side of fort at that moment discovered the advance of the Indians coming up the ravine.

They poured in a heavy fire as soon as they reached the level ground and gained possession of some outbuildings.

Lieutenant Sheehan immediately ordered Lieut. Gere with a detachment to hasten to the point of attack. Whipple brought his howitzer into position between the two buildings. A detachment from Co. C headed by Sheehan moved on the run around the north end of the barracks and took up their position in a row of log buildings in the rear. At the same time McGrew put his howitzer into position at the northwest corner. The howitzers and the musketry fire did the work effectively and the Indians soon abandoned the buildings they had siezed and fell back to the shelter of the ravine. The attempt to take the fort at the first rush had been frustrated. While the attack on the east was going on Little Crow with the rest of his warriors attacked on the west and the south where Sergeant Jones with his trusty six pounder was ready to give them a warm welcome. The battle now became general. For five hours, the firing was incessant but at nightfall the Indians withdrew to the Lower Agency. They had all the battle they wanted in one day. It was enough to last them the next day, too. It was not until Friday that Little Crow could again induce his warriors to endeavor to take the fort. In the meantime a 12-pounder field piece not hitherto used, was manned and put in position in reserve on the parade ground, under command of Sergeant Bishop. During the first day's battle the women and children were collected in the stone barracks. The quarters were none too large and they were packed to the doors and windows with crying children and frightened women. During the firing on the first day, the panic in the barracks was indescribable.

When Little Crow and his yelling blanketed warriors spread themselves over the prairie around the fort at noon on Friday its defenses had been strengthened greatly since the first attack. It was the cunning chief's plan to take the fort with a fierce onslaught. He well knew the character of his warriors. Under his orders they dismounted and left their ponies on the prairie about a mile distant from the fort. Then, with those blood-curdling yells, which are such a characteristic of Indian battles, they closed in on the fort, delivering a rapid fire as they came. Confident in their numbers, the braves exposed themselves, to the very effective fire from the fort and many a fierce warrior fell on the prairie sod and bit the grass in his last agonies. The open advance proving too dangerous for the assailants. Little Crow fell back upon his second plan of firing the garrison by a prolonged and constant fire hoping in the end that another onslaught would be successful. The Indians sought the shelter of the ravines as much as possible, while those on the open prairies, covering their heads and bodies with tufts of prairie grass, wriggled towards the fort giving the prairie the appearance of being alive with unseen animals. Little Crow ordered his brave followers to take possession of the stables and the sutler's building near the southwest corner of the fort. From this cover such a hot fire was poured in that the buildings in that corner were literally riddled with bullet holes. The buildings were shelled to dislodge the Indians and were by the same means fired. While their flames were brightly ascending and the black smoke was hanging over the prairie, already baked by the heat of an August day, the Indians began to shoot burning arrows into the buildings of the fort. But the rain of the previous day had made the roofs so wet that they would not take fire. The attack was now at its height and the scene was appalling beyond description. Flaming arrows whizzing through the sky, burning buildings, death and wounds, the reverberating artillery, and the demoniac yells of the Indians, mingled with the frightened cries of children and the groans of the wounded, made it a moment never to be forgotten.

Lieutenant Sheehan during the fight was present at all points of the garrison cheering his men to victory and directing them to keep up a steady fire but not to waste their ammunition.

To divert attention from the southwest where he proposed to make his final onslaught, Little Crow now directed an especially severe attack against the northeast corner. Whipple, with his gun supported by infantry, under Lieutenant Gere, swept the grass to the roots along the crest of the ravine. The savages fell back and sought the shelter of the earth, but were not given a respite, for the brave McGrew boldly pushed his howitzer out from the northwest corner, to the edge of the ravine and enfilladed its slopes with an effective fire which sent many a bloody handed warrior straight to the happy hunting grounds while the wounded groveled on the ground. Over the edge of the hill fell the shells from Whipple's gun while down the ravine hissed McGrew's enfillading canister.

The writer cannot commend Lieut. T. P. Gere too highly commanding his company, and B. H. Randall commanding the citizens during the siege.

Little Crow, excellent general that he was, saw that the critical moment had now arrived. By means of orders quickly carried by the chief's messengers, among whom was his little son, a general convergence of the Indian forces was made on the southwest. McGrew noticed the changing arrangement of the besiegers, and communicated his knowledge to Sergeant Jones who was acting as chief of artillery. The latter immediately directed him to put in action the 24-pounder field-piece from which not a single shot had yet been fired, and fire on the west line of the fort at the south end of the commissary buildings.

Realizing that cannons were their worst foes, the Indian sharpshooters had exerted themselves to get Sergeant Jones. Every lineal foot of timber along the line of the barricade which protected his gun was splintered by a close and accurate fire. But still the gun was worked and the shells continued to fall among the warriors at the shortest possible range.

McGrew dropped the first shell from the big gun in dangerous proximity to the party that was swinging around from the northeast. Training his gun to the west, he dropped the second shell exactly at the point where this party had joined a group of squaws, ponies and dogs, west of the main body. Yelping dogs, shrieking squaws, wailing children and frightened bucks ran in all directions and sought shelter behind every inequality of the ground. McGrew then directed his fire between this force and the main body and succeeded in preventing a consolidation. The reports of the big gun were as demoralizing to the Indians as its frightful execution.

In the meantime in front of Jones' position there was a lull in the fire, and across the space separating the combatants, the whites could hear Little Crow exhorting his warriors to take courage for the last fierce rush. With all the art of a Webster or a Calhoun, the chief implored, commanded and urged his warriors to take the fort or die in the attempt. While the general of the Indian forces tried the effect of oratory, Jones arranged a very effective counter argument, by double shotting his piece with canister. Spurred on by the inspiring words of the chief, a band of desperate warriors rushed straight towards Jones' barricade. The Indian doesn't always fight behind trees; sometimes he delivers an assault in the open as bravely as white troops. Witness the charge of Roman Nose and his warriors, in the bloody fight with Forsyth. On came the painted, yelling warriors, brandishing their weapons and leaping madly in their rage and hatred. A cloud of smoke belched from the black muzzle of the gun, a band of flame shot forward, and eighteen warriors fell to the ground in the agonies of death or gaping wounds. This terrible blow completely unmanned the savages. They fell back in disorder pursued by shrieking shells thrown through the flame and smoke of the burning buildings. The fight was over. Little Crow hastily collected the wounded and the dead; as far as possible, broke up the camp in the valley and began his retreat. In the silence that followed the dirges chanted for the dead by the weeping Indian women came up from the valley and mingled with the cries of the hysterical women and children in the stone buildings. The moment was too awful even, for shouts of triumph, from the begrimed but the successful defenders of the fort.

Suddenly a strange and weird spectacle caught Lieut. Sheehan's eyes as he glanced up at the smoky clouds. There, in the clouds, occurred a phenomenon that in a more credulous age would have been taken as a sign of grace direct from God himself. On the screen of the clouds, as though thrown by some great stereopticon, a mirage repeated and revealed the whole battle scene. The outline of the fort and the disposition of its defenders was clearly shown with all at their places and the guns still throwing shells into the valley, where the retreating Indians as shown by the images in the clouds, were in the deepest confusion. Teepees were being torn down, goods were being packed on ponies, papooses were strapped to backs, and hurried retreat begun, while the sullen warriors held back to guard the rear. In their turn the Indians could see reflected the confident aspect of all within the fort. It cannot be doubted that to their superstitious minds it was an unmistakable sign of the wrath of the Great Spirit. They redoubled the speed of their flight and westward moving dust clouds announced that the Indian insurrection had passed its zenith. The gate had been tried and had held.

During the six hours in which the Indians raged around like so many furies freed from hell, all the well women in the fort showed the greatest composure. The supply of ammunition for the small arms having been exhausted, Lieut. Sheehan set them to opening spherical case shot to get the powder with which they made cartridges. The missles for these cartridges were supplied by pieces of rod cut up by men especially detailed for the work. It is said that the dismal whistling of these pieces of nails propelled through the air unseen filled the Indians with a great superstitious fear.

During the siege of the fort nine babies were born in the barricade, but only two of them lived. The little garrison, in all the hot fighting lost but five men killed and eighteen wounded. The Indian loss was never known, but from the numbers that were seen to fall, their loss must have been at least 100. Their total number engaged varied from 500 on the day of the first attack to 1500 on the last day.

Five days longer the garrison remained under arms, expecting a renewal of the fight, but on August 27th 175 horsemen under command of Capt. Anson Northrup from Minneapolis reached the fort and all the danger was over. Henceforth the Indians were on the defensive. Well aware of the fate into which their thirst for blood had led them, they scattered over the prairies or surrendered after two or more battles. The stubborn defense of Fort Ridgley turned the tide. Had it not been for the "holding of the gate" as the Indians figuratively put it, the savage war might have been carried to the eastern borders of the state. The honors of this great defense belong to all those who participated in it, but the young Irish lieutenant who marched his company 42 miles in one night, took command of the fort and directed its defense with consummate skill, deserves to go down to history along with those of the most honored commanders in all the years of border warfare. His name should be written side by side with that of Forsyth, Crooks, Custer, Wayne and Jackson. Well does he deserve the bronze medal which adorns his breast.

The facts for this review of the heroic defense of Fort Ridgley have been taken from the narrative of the Fifth regiment compiled by Gen. Lucius F. Hubbard and from statements made to the writer, by Capt. Sheehan. The account of the siege of Fort Ripley in Gen. Hubbard's narrative, was prepared by Lieut. T. P. Gere, second lieutenant in Company B.

The state of Minnesota has erected on the Fort Ridgley battle ground a beautiful monument in honor of Sheehan and the gallant defenders of the fort which speaks to the world with its tongue of bronze, in memory of the fallen, in recognition of the living and for the emulation of future generations.

Erected A.D., 1896, by the state of Minnesota, to preserve the site of Fort Ridgley, a United States military post established in 1853 and especially to perpetuate the names and commemorate the heroism of the soldiers and citizens of the state, who successfully defended the fort during nine days of siege and investment, August 18th to 27th, 1862, and who gallantly resisted two formidable and protracted assaults upon it made August 20th and 22nd, 1862, by a vastly superior force of Sioux Indians, under command of Little Crow and other noted Indian leaders and warriors.

August 18th, 1862, the Sioux Indians of the Upper Minnesota river, in violation of their treaties, broke into open rebellion, and within a few days thereafter, massacred about one thousand citizens in the southwestern part of the state, and destroyed property of the value of millions of dollars. Many men, women and children fled to Fort Ridgley and were under its protection during the siege. The successful defense of the fort by its garrison, consisting of parts of companies B and C Fifth regiment of Minnesota Volunteer Infantry, the "Renville Rangers" and citizens and refugees, was very largely instrumental in saving other portions of Minnesota from ravage and devastation, and greatly contributed to the ultimate defeat of the Indians and their expulsion from the state.

During the entire siege of Fort Ridgley the garrison was skillfully commanded by Lieut. Timothy J. Sheehan, of Company C, Fifth regiment of Minnesota Infantry. He was ably assisted by Lieut. Norman K. Culver, Co. B of the same regiment. Acting Post Quartermaster and Commissary in charge of detachments; Lieut. Thomas P. Gere, Co. B, Fifth Minnesota Infantry, in command of the portion of his company, present (Capt. John F. Marsh and twenty-three men of that company, and Peter Quinn, United States interpreter, having been killed by the Indians at Redwood Ferry Aug. 18th, 1862); Lieut. James Gorman in command of the Renville Rangers; Hon. Benjamin H. Randall, in charge of armed citizens; Ordinance Sergeant John Jones, of the regular army, in general charge of the artillery, with Sergeant James G. McGrew, Co. B, 5th Minnesota Infantry, and Mr. J. C. Whipple, each in charge of a gun. Dr. Alfred Muller, Post Surgeon. The names of the other defenders appear on this monument.

Captain Sheehan and Lieutenant Gere commanding companies "B" and "C" of the Fifth Minnesota Infantry after the Minnesota Massacre were ordered south and joined their regiment near Oxford, Miss., on the 12th day of December, 1862 and served with the regiment to the end of the war.

Incidents

Fool, crazy or brave? Which?

In the year 1868 the Bloods were very troublesome. They would pick off men on the Fort Benton & Helena Road and often attack little outfits. While we were in camp on Sun river we had a little tussle with them. They came within twenty rods of us and commenced to drive off our horses. A few shots were exchanged and one of our boys received a slight wound on the muscle of his arm. None were killed. The enemy captured our horses. One Frank

Murphy purchased a fine mare in Helena which he prized so highly he talked of nothing else; the boys teased him, remarking "she is no good." The Indians took his mare with the rest. The poor fellow was nearly crazy. Had his mother been taken he could have expressed no deeper sorrow. The boys told him to "strike out and recover her." They talked to him till he said he thought he could. In the night he disappeared no one knew where. Had the imbecile gone to try to find their camp, and get his horse back? We remained in camp about four days; on the third day he made his appearance. He was a terrible sight to behold. He said, "I took a little food for lunch and after you retired for the night I started north for the British lines; I travelled all night, struck a trail followed it up and a camp was in sight. This was, I judge, about 9 o'clock A.M. About half a mile from camp I saw a number of ponies. Went up among them and saw two Indian boys driving some towards the camp. I saw mine in the herd; it had no picket line on so I could not catch it easily. I had a halter along, but could do nothing as I had no horse to put it on. Soon out rushed a hundred bucks and surrounded me. They took me to camp. I told them I wanted my horse; they laughed, talked and looked at me. They kept me outside a short time and then they all dispersed. The chief took me into a

ANTELOPE BILL 73

teepee (tent) gave me some pemican (dried meat), and tallow mixed. I ate some, and when they found I had enough, they stripped me of my clothing and sent an escort with me about five miles away and made signs for me to go, which I did. I struck out in a southwesterly direction, arrived at the Sun river and followed it down. He arrived back after a three days' absence. The Indians thought him crazy perhaps, or a fool. They will never take the life of such.

ANTELOPE BILL'S FIRST BUFFALO HUNT

The reader may wish to know how the author came by such a strange wild name as Antelope Bill. For convenience the name Bill was given by the two Boston tourists, on the occasion of the hunt hereafter described and the prefix Antelope, was given by the Indian Renville. Whether I liked the name or not, I was obliged to accept it, and here I make use of it.

In the month of June or July two tourists called at the Sioux agency. They wore good clothing and were well supplied with "funds." They may have been horsethieves, blacklegs, or something worse for aught we knew. They brought no letters of introduction. They evidently had seen little of frontier life. One evening the clerk at the government agency built a fire or smudge to keep off the mosquitoes. Along the streams in the west they are sometimes abundant. We were getting the benefit of the smoke when one of the tourists stepped to the fire and putting up his hands said: "It is quite chilly, is it not?" "Yes," said the clerk "it is quite so." These men were keeping out of the smoke as much as possible. "How thick the mosquitoes are" said one, "Yes, said the other, how is it they don't trouble you fellows over there?"

"Because we keep out of the smoke as much as possible," said the clerk. They saw the intended sarcasm and went into the smoke, but it proved too much for them; they thought the smoke quite as unendurable as the mosquitoes. They remained a few days, taking in the sights. One day an Indian brought in a little Buffalo meat; they got the interpreter to ask where they found buffalo, and were told it was about twenty miles away; they asked many questions, such as these: "How do you kill them? Can they run fast? Would they hook? How large are they? Can you kill them without creeping on them?" I understood the interpreter. He told them they were as tame as sheep. You could knock them down with an axe; they are harmless and can only walk. The tourists apparently gave credence to all that was told them. I knew better for I had seen the Indians in pursuit of two before this, at a short distance from Redwood Falls. They thought it would be fine sport to hunt and kill them; they were told plenty of antelope could be found near by. Many more questions were asked and they expressed a wish to go out and try their luck. The interpreter said Renville would go with them; he could be trusted—he was a Sioux! One of the counties of Minnesota was afterwards named for him. The gents asked as many questions about Renville as about the game, and decided to go on a hunting expedition provided Renville, others and myself would go and insure safety. I was nothing but a beardless boy, but securing the agent's consent I accompanied the party. Little Rock, a Frenchman, who understood Sioux, went with us. Guns were borrowed from the agency. The following morning Renville came around with his two ponies and light wagon. Our luncheon consisted of some flour and salt with some coffee. We started in a northwestern direction and at about eleven o'clock Renville sighted a jack-rabbit; at the same time the tourists saw it and became nearly frantic. I wished to capture the first game. Renville and Rock remained behind while the others of the party started on the chase. We raised two more rabbits which gave one for each in pursuit. These would encourage us to follow along; they would rest until we were within shooting distance, then off they would go. At length I became discouraged; not so the others, they kept on an hour longer, then condemned the guns and not the rabbits. We all got into the wagon and started. We soon saw another before us but the gents and myself were not so eager now for success and we told Renville to try his luck. He got out and went a short distance over a "sag." Soon we heard the report of his gun. Then Renville made his appearance with his rabbit; he said we would have to go about two miles before we could come to water to cook our rabbit. Dinner being over, we started once more. Renville said we would see buffalo before night. We travelled about five miles and sighted antelope at a distance. The gentlemen were now more on the alert than ever. We drove till within eighty rods of them and then halted. The gentry could hardly get from the wagon quick enough; I thought I would not be in very great haste this time. They followed them as they did the rabbits; they circled back towards the wagon. Little Rock and Renville crept down the ravine. Soon they made their appearance on a knoll and taking a red pocket-handkerchief from the pocket and waving it, the antelope began circling around them; each moment as they moved, the circle grew less in circumference. When near enough, Renville fired, and was successful bringing down his game. He motioned to me to drive over, which I did. We loaded the game into the wagon; the secret of the handkerchief they promised not to reveal till after I succeeded in bringing down game—till I had killed an antelope. Wearied out, the party came up; they had fired a dozen shots and still condemned their guns. All aboard once more. After going about two miles further on, we saw more game. I exchanged guns with Rock, requested the party to remain behind and let me try my luck. They consented. Here the ground was very level; I went about twenty rods and pulled out my handkerchief. It was not red; I went back to the wagon and got Rock's. The men were surprised. The secret was out; the game in sight saw my red signal and commenced to move in a circle about me. They came so near I could have hit them with a stone. Now is my time. Bang! They all ran. Soon one dropped. Now I sprang forward to my game. The gentlemen were quite crestfallen because the beardless boy was second best on the trip so far. Said they, addressing me, "Antelope, you are not going to get the next." Rock says, "Bill, if you can only get a buffalo!" About sundown we came to timber near a lake having been moving for about an hour when we discovered a herd of buffalo. Renville explained that some Indians were after them; they kept coming nearer and nearer toward us. We could see the smoke of guns, though not hearing a report. We could also see them dropping one by one. Renville thought he would drive over to where they were. By the time we got to them the last one had been brought down. There were three Indians and they had killed twelve buffalo. Soon other Indians came for the meat, and camping near them enjoyed a square meal (as they were camped near the lake). So also did we. In the Indian camp the women were cutting the meat into strips to dry, hanging it on sticks. There were about twenty dogs around camp. The women were washing roots and putting away for the winter. This expedition was like a new revelation to the tourists and myself. We all retired early to rest first covering with a light blanket, but the wolves and other wild animals kept up such a howling and the dogs in camp such a barking, that none could rest and we were up in the morning as soon as the mud hens in the lake. I remained with the gentlemen in camp, while Rock and Renville mounted ponies to go a distance away and see if there were signs of buffalo. Soon they were over the hills and out of sight. We did not enjoy the thought of being so near neighbors. Soon we had a few callers from the other camp; they wanted flour. The gents gave them what there was in the sack. Soon Rock made his appearance, his pony coming on a full jump. The

ANTELOPE BILL

tourists' countenance changed color quickly. Said Rock: "Boys, there are a 100 buffalo over the hill; Renville is guarding or herding them." (You can drive buffalo, if you do not first frighten them). "Bring your guns and follow me."

Travelling two miles we came to a level plain, and saw what appeared like a herd of cattle. Our tourists were in haste. Rock cautioned them to keep on the windward side as much as possible. One paid no attention to this, but went on pell-mell. Renville was all the time driving them towards us, and got them within 80 rods of us, when the gents commenced to fire and away they went. Renville began shooting, killing three and then came back towards us. I was sitting over on a little rise of ground hoping they would turn and come my way. No. Looking north towards the tourists there were about twenty-five of the herd coming towards them, which, they seeing, "squatted" down, took aim, and bang! bang! their guns went. The herd wheeled and went the other way. Soon a stray bull came along. One of the gents raised his gun and fired; the bull went a few rods and stopped; the gents went toward him and fired, the bull standing still. Renville came along watching the movements of both. All at once the bull rushed forward catching one of the men on his horns holding him slightly; one shot from the gun of Renville hit the animal behind the shoulders and brought him down. These tourists had seen enough and wanted to go back to Boston as soon as possible. We went to camp, hitched to wagon, loaded some meat and drove homeward fast as we could. These tourists were not looking for rabbit or antelope. But oh, the vermin. One of these men was called Buffalo Bill, but he did not fancy the name any more than I that of Antelope Bill. After this they stopped but a short time at the agency and returned to Boston. Poor Rock is now in his grave; he has been through many a hard battle. He served in the First Minnesota Rangers, was a scout, and had many a skirmish with the enemy. He lost his life by marrying a Sioux maiden. An Indian murdered him.

A Visit to Little Crow's Home

A few weeks after my escape from the Indians I went on business to Camp Release, above the Yellow Medicine River. This was the place where the Indians surrendered to Gen. Sibley. I was accompanied by two others. When near Little Crow's village we thought we would go over to his house which was still standing. To our surprise, there lay two Sioux Bucks in their war paint apparently dead. They may be only sleeping. There being many tall weeds about the dooryard they were nearly hidden from sight. My thoughts were, they may be drunk. I dismounted and made sure they would never awaken. I mounted and overtook my companions. I did not dare fire a gun for fear the report would arouse others. A broken rail was my weapon of defense. Their bodies were found and it was said they had been killed by someone.

A Sick Man

Capt. Kimball accompanied us to Ft. Benton. He was an old river captain on the Mississippi and the Missouri rivers. Leaving his boat in care of the mate near Cow Island, Montana. The water in the river was very low. Capt. Kimball, Frank Adams and myself took a stroll trying to get an elk as they were plenty on the bottom lands. We spied a herd and surrounded them. Elk will huddle together when parties approach them from opposite direction. Three Indians have been known to kill twenty from one herd thus huddled together. We needed a little meat and only wished to kill one. I think we killed one apiece. Capt. Kimball not being an expert with a rifle, he over shot and struck a little calf, cutting the skin on its head, making a small ridge and knocking him down. The captain was slow in getting up to him. To secure this game the calf's throat should have been cut; but no, the captain seeing him trying to regain his feet raised him by the neck (the calf crying like a child). His courage failed him; and he would not let it be hurt. It was given its freedom and scampered away to find its mother. We took what meat we wished for and started for camp. We had gone out from the bottom upon the open prairie when to our surprise we were overtaken by a dozen Crow Indians. They came up saying "how how?" (How are you?) We knew we had passed the Sioux country. We knew these Indians were friendly but would steal; would take from us all they could. Knowing they were Crows, I placed too much confidence in them. None of us could speak their language. By signs they invited us to sit down and smoke the pipe of peace with them which we did. When Capt. Kimball's turn came to take the pipe he refused, saying it would make him sick. Being over persuaded, he complied and soon he was "outside" and his breakfast was cast up. The Indians gobbled up our firearms, made us take off our clothing, and taking everything from us told us to get. The captain felt more like staying; we were left without a rag. We all managed to get in sometime in the night.

A Surprise

A refugee from Leavenworth had gone as far as he could. He called at a house; it was deserted. From appearances the occupants had just taken a meal. Nothing showed disturbance. Fowls were about the door, and the cattle on the farm. He had the potatoes on cooking when the door opened and an Indian came marching in saying "how how?" The refugee recognized him as a Winnebago. The Indian said "me hungry," giving the white man his gun telling him "me good Indian; me Winnebago, me going to Sioux." They took supper together. Come to find out this Indian knew nothing of the massacre. He came from the Winnebago agency on the old Indian trail. He wished to stay all night. He was put into a bed and it was but a short time before he was snoring and the refugee was on his way to New Ulm. The Indian was left minus his gun. The refugee found New Ulm surrounded with Indians so he turned about and made for Mankato where in due time he arrived safely.

The Brown Family

Consisting of father and mother, old people of 70 years, a niece, and a son of about thirty years were living on the Cottonwood river. Some one coming up to the door advised them to flee as the Indians were killing the whites. Regarding this as a false alarm, they gave no heed till a second messenger bore the same story. Hastily the young man put the oxen to the wagon. Putting in a feather bed and household conveniences, they started. They had gone only half a mile when they met Indians. The young woman drove the team while father and son took to the side of the wagon determined to sell life as dearly as possible. The father and son were shot down while the poor women were left to their fate. In about two weeks the bodies of these four people were found horribly mutilated within a few rods of each other. The feathers and goods were scattered about.

Sometings Go Buzz-Buzz

We left Fort Benton with fifteen teams and eighteen men including the wagon boss and his assistant for Cow Island in the Missouri river. We went for freight. The river was low and the boats could go no further up. The distance to be gone over was about one hundred and seventy-eight miles and directly through the Sioux the Crow and the "blood country." Indians all the way. I hired out as night herder, riding in the day time and herding the cattle at night. I had a pony, rifle, and two revolvers. For about a hundred miles the country is rather mountainous, and the balance is somewhat rolling. Very little timber is found on the streams. We carried sufficient fuel for cooking purposes for three days near the vicinity of Milk river. We came upon some Crow Indians, who were friendly; they always were to the whites, only they are

ANTELOPE BILL 85

such inveterate thieves. We passed near their camp and stopped for dinner; they came to us and such a sight as they presented. On closer observation we were convinced they had smallpox. We had visited their camp; that was enough. In their teepees were old and young lying in a helpless condition. Many of the men had left women and children; had deserted. We left hastily but were told no white man would take the disease from an Indian. It proved true in our case. These Indians caught the disease from a blanket they had stolen from a boat going up the Missouri river. We arrived at Cow Island having no more trouble with Indians. We found the boat well loaded and a few passengers for the mountains. After three days we started back well loaded; we took three men with us leaving the rest for other work. Another man was put with me to herd, also a German who could speak little English, to watch at night. The teamsters slept within the enclosure as the Indians might attack us. About the fifth day out I was sitting in front of the wagons watching the antelope. At a distance I saw an object and called the teamster's attention to it. He said he thought it was elk. I said it was an Indian and he would make his appearance again at night. I suggested to the boss wagoner that a guard should be placed on duty at night. The horses and cattle were brought closer together that they might not be stolen. The boys sat up late by a little fire telling stories until about 11 o'clock and at twelve, I went to the enclosure to get a lunch. The German was at the gape bending close over the fire to get the benefit of the few coals that remained. I cautioned him telling him there were Indians about. I pointed to a sag and told him the Indians would come—not walking, but crawling. I inquired of him if he understood. He said "yaw, yaw." I ate my lunch, sharing it with Jim Cook. We laid on the ground talking; in a little while our cattle started off and we drove them in again. We laid down again. Soon we heard our German yell "Inches! Inches!" We rushed to him. The teamsters started up, but nothing was to be seen only our German, and the blood running down his face. We gathered around him and he said "somedings come buzz, buzz" pointing to his forehead, at the same explaining to me that he sat in the enclosure near the coals with his face toward the ravine. His face was pale and he looked scared. We knew something was wrong. Search was made and within ten feet of where he was sitting an arrow was found sticking in the ground, about four inches having been left above. The Indians had crept up the ravine to a wagon and standing up had fired hoping to kill, by fixing the arrow in his temple and then to get the horses that were inside. The German afterwards refused to stand guard.

Minus One Ear

The diamond train was known in the early days in Montana with its trail of three wagons drawn by six yoke of oxen. The drivers whips would pop and sound like a discharge of guns in those deep canons. The teamsters that accompanied this trip to Cow Island on the Missouri river, were a jolly set. The writer relates a few instances that happened on the last trip for that season of 1869. Nothing of importance happened on their way down, the boys simply becoming noisy at intervals on account of a little too much tangle foot. The boys being well supplied, we waited on the island for a few days letting the teams rest in the meantime and to load the wagons. When loaded and rested we returned home with less whiskey and in its place an abundance of meat consisting of buffalo, elk, and antelope. Why should we not be a jolly set of ox punchers of the Northwest? In a few days the scales turned, the wagon boss a little fatigued by being in the saddle so much, often exchanged with the boys; this is the case I am about to relate: John Anson mounted his horse taking his Springfield musket, and strapping his large Colt's revolver to his waist, took his departure in advance and over the rolling prairie thinking he might add one more antelope to swell the meat supply. Putting the spurs to the broncho he was soon out of sight over the small hills and ravines. Going about one mile he saw two leisurely feeding. John stopped his horse, and eying them considered the best way to sneak on them: While doing so, his horse turned his head around to the south John looking the same way. Sure enough; there were two Indians riding towards him. Seemingly they had come out of the ground not forty rods away. Coming directly towards him they halted, at the same time beckoning John to come where they were. He did so without a second thought. They saluted with the friendly how-how, one extending his left hand to John, he extending his right, giving the Indian a good shake. Same time Mr. (lo) pulled his revolver with his right and taking aim fired. John fell from his horse the Indians catching it, leading it off not caring to molest the dead man or his firearms, they had gone only a few rods when John raised up and fired. One dropped from his horse; he fired again. Mr. (lo) firing about the same time and taking his quick departure was out of sight.

John caught the extra pony and robbed the corpse of his scalp, knife and firearms, coming to us minus one ear, one side of his face black with burnt powder, and left side covered with blood. On investigation the Indian supposed he had shot him through the head which was their intention, they being in a hurry for fear the rest of the boys were coming towards them.

This little excitement soon blew over; nothing more occurring until we came to the Sun River. Here we camped for a couple of days on account of the teams straying off, which took a number of the boys from camp and others were out sporting, as ducks and grouse were plenty.

Being out of the Sioux country, the boys could roam where they chose to, as these Indians were Black Foots and Bloods; not bad and bloodthirsty. Sometimes if they saw a man out by himself they would kill him; oftentimes they were impudent, especially in large numbers, an instance of which I will mention. Three of our boys were in camp, the cook preparing the dinner, when up rode a war party and dismounted, stating they were going down to the Sioux country after scalps as they were enemies to the Sioux. Soon they made their wants known by telling us they wanted something to eat. Their wish was granted by giving them a little flour, bacon and sugar also coffee. They were not satisfied with that but wanted it cooked; this we refused to do for so large a crowd. They instantly became angry and it appeared as though there would be trouble. During these few moments of controversy two of the boys managed to get hold of their muskets; the cook kept at his cooking as though nothing had or would happen, but his good disposition was riled by a saintly red stepping up and spitting a chew of tobacco in the fryingpan of meat. About the same time Mr. Buck was biting dust between the wagon wheel, the two other boys had their two Indians covered with their muskets, telling them to "get" as luck was with us. Some of the other boys showed up at a short distance and away they went as fast as their ponies could carry them. The cook has scolded himself mad many a time, because he did not serve him in the face as he did in the frying-pan.

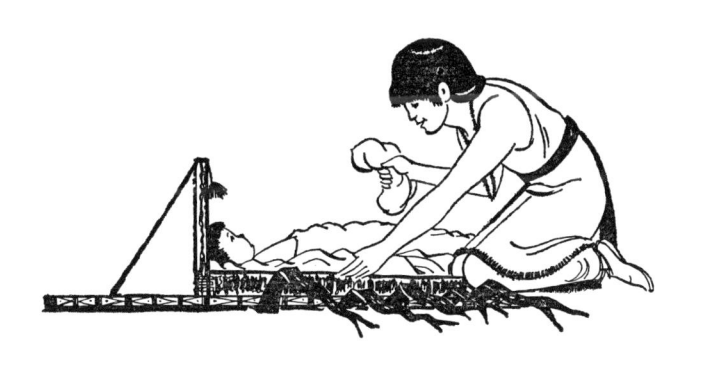

Horses Tails Made Use of Many Ways

How two or three Indians will travel a great distance in one day is thus illustrated: The writer has known them to travel over 75 miles a day; it is done in this way. When two or three are making a journey, and they are poor, having only one pony, one will catch hold of his tail while the others ride astride on the animal's back; when he becomes somewhat fatigued it is reversed by changing around. The pony is picketed out and let rest about every ten miles for about half an hour, then they continue their journey. They never approach a horse when they want to catch him but catch him by the tail; then he will stand perfectly still. Sometimes he may whirl around and then give up; he will never kick.

The writer, recollects when travelling with some Red river half-breeds, they had their carts and came to a ravine which was very steep; the ponies tried very hard to pull the load up, but soon became discouraged. One of the men dismounted, tied a knot in the horse's tail and put him ahead of the cart using rawhide as rope was not to be had, winding and tying it to the knot then back to the thill; the whip and word was given, and up the hill they went; they claim a horse will pull more by the tail than by the shoulders.

The writer has seen them in battle, when one was wounded, being shot from his horse, manage to get hold of the pony's tail and he dragged off the battle ground. Sometimes a warrior will ride up to a wounded man, catch the horse's tail, and is dragged off, saving his life and scalp.

The Killing of the Jewett Family Near Mankato

In the month of August, 1865, a few miles out from Mankato there resided a family by the name of Jewett consisting of Mr. Jewett and wife and young babe; their aged father and mother, and the hired man. Mr. Jewett was a well-to do farmer. He had just returned from the army bringing with him the amount of money saved—about three hundred dollars. In the same company there was a half-breed by the name of Campbell. He had always been friendly to Mr. Jewett. After being discharged they separated, Mr. Jewett coming to his family and farm at Mankato and Campbell to his brothers at Le Sueur or near there. There had been considerable excitement about Mankato as Indians had been seen. A boy and soldier had been killed and people were on the lookout— were apprehensive of mischief. A Mr. Stevens was taking a walk up the Blue Earth river. Walking leisurely along he met a suspicious looking fellow. He arrested him and took him to Mankato. When he arrived at the town the news of the murder of the Jewett family had just reached there. The prisoner was placed in close confinement until the matter was examined. Parties went from Mankato to the place where the tragedy had been committed. They found blood stained walls and floors; the old gentleman was just alive. The young babe by its mother was somewhat hurt but recovered. The old gentleman was able to tell the story. It appears that Campbell and five Indians visited the place. Campbell came for the money, and the Indians for blood. Campbell was visited in jail by a priest and other parties and after a time made a confession. He acknowledged having on Mr. Jewett's pants and stockings. He told where the money was secreted. His life ended by being suspended from a tree growing near where the State Normal school building now stands. The Indians were pursued west and overtaken near what is now Lyon County; four were shot and the bones of the other were found afterwards near by.

The Capture by the Sioux in 1862 of John Schurch a Lad of 15

The author met him at his home in Minneapolis and talked over our boyhood days in territorial times at Mankato, Minn. We served in the same regiment, have met each other often and not knowing this was the nervy John who is now a resident and business man of Minneapolis.

With the gradual disappearance of the Indian tribes which, but a short time ago roamed at will in the virgin wilderness, since reclaimed and devoted to the uses of civilization, interest in their doings is swallowed up and overshadowed by the interests and pursuits of the present day. It is difficult, indeed, for one to imagine, especially one not to the manner born, that it is now only a few years since the Sioux and Chippewas disputed for the supremacy within a few miles of Minneapolis. But such is the fact. And while the Sioux are considered the most warlike of the Northern tribes, they usually came off second best in their frequent fights with the Chippewas. The Sioux have, nevertheless, impressed themselves and their history indelibly forever by the massacre of 1862, that great tragedy which shook the whole nation to its profoundest depths, even though an unparalleled civil war was raging in another part of the country. The principal features of that sanguinary time are still remembered by Minnesotans of middle age, but there are many details that have never been related; among them, and probably the most interesting of all being the capture of then a boy of fifteen, now a man of fifty engaged in business in Minneapolis, and very well known to thousands of people in both Minneapolis and St. Paul. Yet few would imagine that this modest man had passed through a more terrific experience for about eleven months than the majority of men pass through in a lifetime. But such is the case however, and Johnny Schurch still lives a voucher for the truth of the narrative.

John Schurch came to Minnesota from Europe in July, 1857. His father had died, and his mother had remarried. The family first settled in Mankato where they stayed two years. They went thence to New Ulm where they remained until 1860, when John's father took up a homestead in Beaver Falls, Renville county, and here the family settled down with the intention of remaining. Early in 1862 the hero of this narrative secured employment as a cook for a gang of six men, who were getting out lumber at Big Stone Lake. Everything ran along smooth here until August 23d, when there appeared in the camp before daylight, an Indian doctor, who warned the crew that the Indians had risen in the lower country; massacred all the whites, and would be at the camp in a few hours. The men scouted the idea, and young Schurch proceeded with preparations for breakfast. Thinking it possible there might be some truth in the medicine man's intelligence all the figles were examined and the men jokingly alluded to their desire for a brush with the "reds." They were not kept long waiting. Schurch had proceeded down to the lake to get a pail of water, when a light rain began. He looked up toward the bluff just above the camp and saw about seventy-five mounted Indians coming over at the same time unrolling their blankets from their guns (having had them rolled in the blankets to keep them dry). Quicker almost than thought there were several sharp reports and five of the six men in camp were writhing in their death agony. To scalp them was only the work of a minute or two, and then began the work of destruction. There were four steers in the camp; two of these were easily captured by the Indians, the others were so wild they had to be shot. Wagons, tents and shanties were burned, and then a search was begun for young Schurch and Anthony Manderfield, both of whom were known by the Indians to be at the camp; but Manderfield had got clean away, and as it subsequently transpired was eleven days going to New Ulm, where he found only the ruins of his former home. As for Schurch, he lay low on the bank of the lake for two hours, seeing all that was going on in the camp seeing his late comrades scalped and their bodies mutilated, listening to the talk of the Indians, but himself unseen. At the end of two hours having completed the work of destruction and feasted to their heart's content, they finally gathered up their traps and departed. It was then only that the now thoroughly frightened lad ventured from his hiding place and penetrated into the deep woods. He came to a group of wild plum trees, thickly covered with grape vines. Here he lay down to evolve a plan of action. He was one hundred and fifty miles from home, alone, surrounded by a tribe of hostile savages, thirsting for his blood. Twice they passed his hiding place within a dozen feet of him and, said he, relating his experience to the writer, "my heart beat so hard it almost made a hole in the ground under me." About noon, as near as he could judge, everything being quiet, he concluded to reconnoitre. He remembered that up at Louis Robert's trading store a short distance away, was a Sioux half-breed clerk, named Baptiste LeClaire. This breed had always been friendly with young Schurch, and he thought if he could communicate with him he would be safe. He approached the log shanty in which Robert's stock was kept and just as he got to the door, Standing Buffalo (Tatonka Naji) chief of the Sisseton Sioux, emerged. Fortunately young Schurch and his family had frequently fed Standing Buffalo and his family, and the chief, without a word, stooped and picked up the lad, wrapped his blanket around him, and held him to his breast. A young Buck in the store who had seen the operation, raised his rifle to fire, when Standing Buffalo commanded him to stop. Just then three Bucks came from behind the building, and were also about to fire on the lad; but the chief still stood his friend, and so, temporarily saved his life. The band rifled the store of such goods as they wanted, and burned the rest, then returned to camp, where the bodies of the five woodsmen still lay exposed in the bush. Here they lay for three days, when the odor became too offensive for

ANTELOPE BILL

the sensitive nostrils of the asthetic Bucks, and the bodies were thrown on a pile of brush and burned. Young Schurch, though kindly treated by Standing Buffalo, was in constant danger from the young men of the tribe, who were one and all very much interested in seeing his scalp dangle from their belt. One day the lad ventured with some Indian children across the creek in search of grapes, and was returning when a young Sisseton Sioux, armed with a long old-fashioned horse-pistol, drew a bead on him and pulled the trigger. The pistol did not go off. The Buck deliberately put more powder on the flint and the little urchin sank in the grass, put his hands over his eyes so as not to see the flash, and awaited his death. The Indian fired, the ball entering Johnny's abdomen, which passed through and nearly came out at the back. The medicine man of the tribe examined him, felt the bullet just beneath the skin, took an old razor which he had looted somewhere, and cut into the lad's back and pried out the bullet with a stick! How this poor lad suffered for the next few weeks, how it was necessary to constantly watch him to save him from the knives or bullets of the Bucks who were constantly trying to dispatch him even while he was lying helpless in the teepee, no words can express. He was in hourly danger of assassination and he knew it. He was alive, yet momentarily expecting death. Who can paint the horror of his situation? Is the cunning of the novelist, the imagination of the most skilled writer equal to the task? Let either essay it, and then retire discomfited. Even imagination has a limit, beyond which practical experience not infrequently advances. The tribe which was being almost daily augmented in numbers, until about a thousand Indians had centered at the spot, remained till late in October. They spent their time in war dances, and in bewailing the fate of the braves who perished from time to time. Young Schurch knew from the black looks fixed upon him from time to time that his life was not worth a moment's purchase if the chief should withdraw his protection. As it was, he was fired at not less than a dozen times between August and October, and says it was nothing less than a miracle his life was spared. Standing Buffalo desired to adopt him into the tribe; by his orders Johnny's face was painted in different colors, his hair was allowed to grow, and the Indian girls braided it and graced the braids with otter tails. He was made herder of the chief's ponies, and received some distinctive marks of Standing Buffalo's favor. But the Bucks jealously watched the opportunity to wipe him out. Once his hat was knocked off his head by a bullet; then his ear was clipped by another: thus it went from day to day, the poor child being kept continually in a state of most dreadful suspense. He did not care for death, he said, but to have it constantly looking for a chance to "jump" him through the agency of a treacherous Sioux was a hell on earth. Finally the tribe concluded to go into winter quarters, and late in October started for the Missouri. They arrived at the site now occupied by Bismarck, after a three week's march subsisting along the route on geese, ducks, wild turnips, etc. The tribe was joined at Apple Creek, (Bismarck) by Little Crow's tribe of 500, and two little white boys, prisoners, and the Yanktons, 2,000, making a total of 3,500, all of whom went into camp for the winter. The Indians occupied their time hunting buffalo and deer; the squaws did all the work. Young Schurch was allowed to mingle with the other little fellows whose parents had been killed, and he was comparatively safe as long as he remained in sight of Standing Buffalo. But just as soon as he ventured among Little Crow's band, or the Yanktons, just so sure was he to experience the hum of a bullet, or be given an opportunity to dodge a whizzing tomahawk. Once hit it would have been "all day" with him, for a score of scalping knives would have flashed in the twilight and a score of braves would have jumped for his scalp. The luck, providence or whatever it was, that preserved him thus far still continued to preserve him, and he escaped. During the winter, about 180 Bucks were selected from the three tribes, and placed under command of Little Crow, who started for Manitoba to effect a coalition with the Crees and other Canadian Northwest tribes for the purpose of organizing a grand raid in the spring of '63 which had for its object the recapture from the whites of all the land between the Missouri river and St. Paul, a prominent feature of which was to be a grand massacre and plunder. The scheme was a grand one and well calculated to appeal to all the instincts of the Canadian Indians. Young Schurch was taken with these envoys extraordinary. After travelling several days the band came in sight of the teepees of the Crees. Ten Sioux scouts were sent ahead to reconnoitre, and little Johnnie was sent with them. A couple of Crees mounted, came out and shook hands with the Sioux. Then four more followed and went through the same operation. Half a dozen Crees then darted out of their camp, circled around the Sioux, gradually contracting the distance, and, when within a hundred yards opened fire on them. This caused a stampede. The Sioux saw the Crees intended to kill them if possible, and they broke for cover. Standing Buffalo was shot in the arm, and the hero of this story received a bullet in the left leg. This ended the "treaty" and the 180 Sioux returned to the Missouri river where they reported the result of their mission. The next day the three branches of the Sioux separated, the Sissetons going to Devil's Lake, and Little Crow's band and the Yankton's proceeding down the river.

"Of course you had a romance?" the writer suggested. "Romance!" Mr. Schurch replied: "I wasn't feeling very romantic just then; I was as thin as a rail, almost constantly suffering from wounds; I was in hourly danger of assassination and never had enough to eat. I know these dime novel heroes usually marry an Indian princess, but they don't do it in real life. I may say, however, that I slept between two squaws all winter to keep from freezing to death. In the morning my hair would be frozen to the side of the teepee, and I had to loosen it the best way I could."

The tribe remained at Devil's Lake from April 1863, to June of the same year, when a Catholic priest from the Canadian side, Father Andrew, appeared in the camp and effected the release of young Schurch and the other lads for a pony each. The United States government had offered four hundred dollars each to any one who would effect the release of any white captive held by the Sioux. This sum was subsequently paid to Father Andrew.

When young Schurch was released and delivered to two halfbreeds to convey to St. Joseph near Pembina, all the Indians gathered in a circle to shake hands with him. When he came to the Buck who had shot him through the bowels, he refused to shake hands with him, and in a short time the three lads started with the two halfbreeds for St. Joseph. They had not proceeded far when one of the breeds looking over his shoulder discerned a cloud of dust. Fearing some treachery, and having noticed young Schurch's refusal to shake hands with one of the Sioux Bucks, they hid the lad in a swamp. Presently about two dozen Indians overhauled the wagon and asked for little Schurch. The breeds told them he had gone on ahead hunting. They lingered however for an hour, and finally begging some tobacco, rode back to their camp. Young Schurch and the party arrived at St. Joseph safely. Father Andrew had the halfbreeds take him to the bank of the Mouse river and give him a thorough scrubbing. Then his hair which came to his shoulders was cut off, and he was dressed in a corduroy suit. As soon as a half breed expedition was ready to start for St. Cloud he was sent with them where he embarked on one of Burbank's stages, and reached St. Paul, only to find that part of his family had been massacred at New Ulm; his mother who was blind, had died of grief; his eldest sister had been butchered by the Indians, and another remained in captivity; she was, however, released in due time, and now resides in South Minneapolis and carries to this day the mark of the tomahawk on her back showing where the Indians had maltreated her. She frequently saw two Indians take a babe, and each taking a leg pull it apart and then dash its brains out against a tree. She saw women have their clothing torn from them, and saw them dreadfully mutilated, hacked with tomahawks and scalped; and a thousand other things she saw, too dreadful for repetition, but the slightest of them cause one to have some of the realizing sense, of the blessings of the present, secure as we are in the possession of a lasting piece—knowing as we do, that the war-whoop of the Sioux will be heard no more forever, on the beautiful, plains of Minnesota, and that the husbandman may pursue his avocations in peace, and the mother need fear no more that the crowing of her baby boy will be followed by the dreadful yell of the savage come to destroy in an hour the fruit of years of labor and the lives which are to her more precious than the breath that sustains her.

Looking at the hero of this narrative, now a prosperous Minneapolis business man, the father of a worthy family, the possessor of most rugged health, and owning a charming home around which all the domestic affections center, it is difficult to believe that this man, now in the very prime and pride of life has passed through such a trying ordeal. But such are the facts. The man is here in person as a living evidence. And we may imagine there are times when evening shadows fall, that he calls up the ghosts of these dead and buried times and looks back upon them with a sort of tender melancholy, because, despite his dangers he passed safely through. Many of the braves who took part in his capture, and others of the opposing tribes who tried in vain so many times to wear his scalp at their belts, have passed to the happy hunting grounds. But few, alas! of all the whites who were among the active spirits of those brave old days remain upon the stage of action. Yet among them all, there is no more cheery, gallant and generous son of Minnesota than little Johnny Schurch, the last survivor of the Sioux captives of 1862.

REMARKS CONCERNING THE SAVAGES
OF THE NORTHWEST

A few exceptions will be made in the remarks by the writer. He admits they are possessed of some good traits as well as bad ones. Savages, we call them, because their manners and customs differ from ours, which we believe to be perfection. Of civility, they think the same of theirs, perhaps if we could examine the manners and customs of different nations with impartiality, we would find no people so rude as to be without any rules of politeness, nor any so polite as not to have some remains of rudeness. The Indian men when young are hunters and warriors, and when old are councilors. All their government is the ruling or advice of sages. No force is used by officers to compel obedience or inflict punishment; and no prisons. They study oratory, and the best speakers take the lead. The Indian women till the ground, dress the food, nurse and bring up the children and preserve and hand down to posterity the memory of public transactions. These employments of the men and women are considered natural and honorable. They have but few artificial wants and thus have abundance of leisure for improvement in conversation. Our laborious manner of life as compared with theirs is esteemed slavish and base and the education with which we value ourselves, they regard as frivolous and useless. An instance of this occurred at a treaty in the west a number of years ago between the Gov't and the Sioux. After the principal business was settled the commissioners acquainted the Indians in a speech "that there were colleges in the East where their children could be educated free of charge to them, and that if the chiefs of the Sioux would send half a dozen of their sons to these colleges, they would be educated, the government taking care that they would be well provided for and be instructed in all the educational branches of white people.

It is one of the Indian rules of politeness not to answer a public proposition the same day it is made. They regard it as treating the matter light; they show respect by taking time to consider it. They defer their answer till the day following.

The speaker began by expressing his deep sense of kindness of our government in making that offer. "We know, that you esteem the kind of learning taught in your colleges, but while caring for our children would be very expensive to you. We are convinced that you mean to do us good by your proposal, and thank you heartily. But you who are so wise, must know that different nations have different conceptions of things, and you will therefore not take it amiss if our ideas of this kind of education happen not to be the same with yours. We have some experience of it. Several of our young men were formerly educated at your colleges; instructed in all of your books and when they came back to us they were bad, ignorant of living on our prairies, could not stand the cold or hunger; complained of our food, would quarrel with the other young men, would lie, could not build a teepee, and could not kill a deer or an enemy. Spoke our language imperfectly. Were therefore neither fit for hunters, lawyers or counsellors. Were totally good for nothing. If you will send a dozen of your sons we will take care of their education, instruct them in all we know and make men of them. See, our men look healthy—they can eat; look at our women, they can work. Send them all up here and we will educate them. Having frequent occasion to visit their open councils with the whites they have acquired great order and decency in conducting them. The old men sit in a circle the women and children on the outside. The business of the women is to take exact notice of what is said and pass imprint of it on their memories. They have no writing as we have; they can communicate it to their children—the records, the council, and they preserve traditions of what happened years and years ago. He who speaks, rises. The rest observe a profound silence. When he has finished and sits down, they leave him five or ten minutes to recollect if he has ommitted anything he intended to say or if he has anything to add, he may rise again and deliver it. To interrupt another, even in common conversation is recorded indecent. How different it is from our Americans. The politeness of these savages is carried to excess; It does not permit them to contradict or deny the truth of what is asserted in their presence. By this means they avoid disputes. But it becomes difficult for anybody to know their minds or what impression you make on them. The missionaries who have attempted to convert them, all complain of this as one of the greatest difficulties of their mission. The Indians hear with patience the truths of the gospel explained to them and give their usual tokens of assent and approbation. You would think they were convinced. A minister having assembled the chiefs, made a sermon to them acquainting them with the principal historical facts on which our religion is founded—such as the fall of our first parents by eating an apple and the coming of Christ to repair the mischief; his miracles, etc. When he had finished an Indian orator stood up. "What you have told us is all very good; it is bad to eat apples; it is much better to make them into cider. We are very glad for you to come so far to tell us those things you have heard from your mothers. In return I will tell you of some things we have heard from ours. In the beginning our fathers had only the flesh of animals to eat and if their hunting was unsuccessful, they were starving. Two of our young men made a fire in the woods. They had killed a deer and cut some off to roast and when they were about to satisfy their hunger they saw a beautiful young woman descend from the clouds, and seat herself on yonder hill which you see there. The young men said to each other "it is a spirit that perhaps has smelt our cooking deer and wishes to eat of it; let us offer some to her." They gave her the tongue and she was pleased with the taste of it, and said "your kindness shall be rewarded. Come to this place after thirteen moons and you will find something that will be a great benefit to you" They did so, and found plants they had never seen before. Where her right hand rested on the ground, there grew corn, and and where here left hand touched it there grew beans and where she sat there grew tobacco. The good missionary disgusted with this idle talk, said "what I have told you are sacred truths; what you tell me are mere fables and lies." The Indian replied: "It seems your friends have not done you justice in your education, they have not well instructed you in the rules. Why do you not believe all of our stories? When any of you come to our camps you are apt to crowd around us and look at us when we wish to be private. This shows the want of instruction." The missionary gave it up as a bad job. An interpreter gave the writer the following: He had been naturalized among the Sioux, and spoke well the Sioux language. In going through the Indian country to carry a message he called at a camp of Sioux to see an old acquaintance who embraced him, and laid furs for him to sit on, gave him some boiled buffalo meat and broth; when he had eaten he lit his pipe, and the friend began to converse with him asking him how he had fared the many moons they had been separated. What occasioned his visit, etc. The interpreter answered all questions and when the discourse began to flag, the Indian said "you have lived long among white people, and know some of their customs. I have been sometimes at St. Paul and observe that once in seven days they close up the stores, and assemble in a great house; tell me what it is; what do they do there? They meet to hear and learn good things. I do not doubt, said the Indian that they tell you so; they tell me the same thing. I doubt the truth of what they say. I will tell you my reasons. I went lately to St. Paul to sell my skins and to buy blankets, knives and powder. You know I used to trade with Roberts but I was a little inclined this time to try some other trader. I called first upon Roberts and asked him how much he would give for beaver. He said he could not give more than 50 cents a pound; "but says he I cannot talk on business now as it is Sunday when we meet to learn about good things, and I am going to meeting." I thought as long as I could not do business I would go to meeting too and I went with him. There stood up a man in black and he began to talk to the people very angrily; I did not understand what he said but perceiving that he looked much at me and at Roberts, I thought he was mad at seeing me there so I went out, sat down near the house and lit my pipe, waiting until the meeting broke up. I thought too, that the man had told about the beaver; I suspected it might be the subject of their meeting; so when they came out I spoke to Roberts. I hope you have concluded to give me more than 50 cents a pound. No, says he, I cannot afford to give more than 30. I then spoke to several other traders but they all sang the same song. This made my suspicions clear and right and whatever they pretended of meeting to learn good things the purpose was to consult how to cheat the Indian in the price of beaver. Consider, but a little, friend, and you will be of my opinion. If they meet so often to learn of good things, they would have learned some before this time, but they are still ignorant. You know our practice is, if a white man is travelling through our country, and enters one of our teepees, to treat him as I do you; we dry him if he is wet, warm him if he is cold, and give him meat if he is hungry and we spread soft furs for him to sleep on and we demand nothing in return. But if I go into white man's house in St. Paul, and ask for something to eat or drink, they say "where is your money?" and if I have none, they say "get out you Indian dog." You see they have not learned those little good things that we need in meetings to be instructed because our mothers taught them to us when we were children, and there-

ANTELOPE BILL

fore it is impossible their meetings should be as they say, for any such purpose, or have any such effect. They are only for the purpose of continuing to cheat the Indian in the price of beaver.

BATTLES OF BIRCH COOLIE AND WOOD LAKE REMINISCENCES OF THE INDIAN WAR

In June 1862, when "Father Abraham" called for 300,000 more men, H. B. Wilson was professor of mathematics in Hamline University, located at Red Wing, Minnesota. Being the only one of three brothers who was physically fitted to endure the hardships of a soldier's life, he conscientiously believed it to be his duty to offer his services to his country and to aid in subduing the rebellion against our government then raging in our southern states. Accordingly at the close of a Friday afternoon's exercises, in the old chapel, to the students, he stated publicly to them what his convictions of duty were, and that he had determined to enlist as a private in a company then forming in the city for the Sixth regiment of Minnesota volunteer infantry. At the same time he invited any of the students present, who might feel so disposed, to enlist with him. Eighteen of the students promptly signified their willingness to join him.

The company was in due time filled to the maximum of 104 men, and left Red Wing on Sunday afternoon August 17th, 1862, on the same boat with Capt. Williston's company, raised for the Seventh Minnesota regiment in the same town. The boat arrived at the mouth of the Minnesota river the next morning at sunrise and the two companies marched into Fort Snelling. We all expected that in a very few days we would take our departure for Virginia to help swell the ranks of McClellan's army of the Potomac. All were animated with patriotism and felt their bosoms swell with an enthusiastic desire to be led at once against the foe. Monday was spent in being examined by the post surgeon to ascertain who of us were sound, and possessed of sufficient muscle, and other requisite qualifications to fit us for soldiers. On Tuesday, the company elected its officers; no ballot was had, but the ceremony was performed by acclamation! and very soon gotten through with. On the evening of the same day, Aug. 19th, a messenger arrived, posthaste, from Fort Ridgley with the exciting news of the outbreak at the Redwood agency, and the massacre of the whites at that place. Our fond dreams of the sunny south and the army of old Virginia were soon dispelled. We were forthwith ordered to prepare ourselves, and be in readiness to start for the frontier by daylight of the next morning. The night preceding our departure was a sleepless one to us all; and was spent in drawing clothing, four days' rations of raw pork and hard tack, and such scanty articles of cooking utensils as we were fortunate enough to find about the garrison. Before it was fairly light on the morning of the 20th, four companies of the Sixth regiment, viz: Co. A., Capt. Grant; Co. B Capt. Merriam; Co. C Capt. Bailey; Co. F Capt. Wilson, under command of Col. H. H. Sibley, embarked on a small steamer and at once started up the Minnesota river. At Shakopee the boat was detained till the next day for the purpose of giving the men an opportunity for obtaining arms and ammunition. A worthless lot of worn-out Belgian muskets were issued to the men, the calibre of which did not correspond in size with the cartridges we obtained. That night Co. F slept on the stone paved levee at Shakopee in a drenching rainstorm without tents, or any shelter, save the canopy of heaven. Many of the men who had so recently left the comforts of home life, and had never previously had any experience in roughing it, began to think that soldiering was not so funny a thing, after all. The next morning we reembarked and proceeded on up the river. The whole country was in a state of the most intense excitement. All along the valley of the Minnesota we constantly met people from the frontiers fleeing from their homes in terror from the savages, whom they imagined were pursuing them, and in their panic believed to be not far behind them. The evening we were at Shakopee some boys who had been out in the woods just back of town hunting cows came in, terror stricken, saying the woods were alive with Indians, that they had heard them halo. As the boat was slowly winding its way up the crooked river, it was frequently met by people descending in skiffs, and on rafts who had the most frightful tales of murders, scalpings and burnings to relate. Just before arriving at Carver, we met two men in a canoe, who said, just as they left there, the mail carrier had just arrived from Glencoe, who brought the news, that the town was on fire, the people had all been either killed, or captured and carried away prisoners by the Indians. At Carver Co. A disembarked and was ordered to march to Glencoe. Capt. Grant, after proceeding to that place and ascertaining that all was quiet, rejoined his command a few days afterwards, at St. Peter. The other three companies left the boat at Belle Plain, and went into camp in the village. That was the first time we slept in tents. The next day, the 23rd, we marched to St. Peter where we remained several days awaiting supplies, and reinforcements. While we were waiting for Col. Sibley's

ANTELOPE BILL 119

troops to get together. Let us take a hasty glance at the events that had transpired at Redwood, Fort Ridgley, New Ulm, and the surrounding section of country.

It may be well, also to inquire for a moment, into the causes that led the Indians to become, just at that time incensed against the whites. In calling attention to these topics it must necessarily be done briefly. The subject is a large one and to treat it with anything like justice would require a volume instead of being confined to the compass of a few pages.

The principal grievances complained of by the Indians were as follows: First, the corruptions in the Indian department that had the management of the distribution of the government annuities. Second, the extortion of the traders. Third, the sufferings of the Indians. Fourth, the prohibition of our government of their sanguinary wars upon the Chippewas. To them this appeared a tyranical act. The hostilities arising from these causes were but trivial in comparison with those which arose out of the sale of their lands and the treaties therewith connected. All who have read the account of the interview between Gov. Ramsey and the Indian Chief Red Iron at the council in 1852, will remember how intensely the Indians were excited at a fraudulent treaty, as they claimed.

Their sufferings from hunger were often severe especially during the winter and spring previous to the massacre. This was owing to the lightness of the crop for the cut worms destroyed all the corn of the Sissetons, and greatly injured that of the other tribes. Then the wild Indians were very much incensed at the abandonment by the farmer Indians of their ancient customs, their assumption of the white dress, and adhesion to the Christian religion.

The dissatisfaction thus engendered was fearfully augmented by the failure of the government to make the annual payment which had before taken place in June, and by the traders refusing them credit at a time when they needed it, the most. They were informed by the traders as a reason of their not trusting them, that it was doubtful on account of the difficulties the government had to encounter, to sustain itself, whether they would receive more than half a payment during the year, and that payment would probably be the last.

In June a number of chiefs and head men of the Sissetons and Wahpetons visited the Upper Agency, and inquired about the payment, whether they were going to get any money, saying they had been told they would not. When the agent informed them that it would take place although he could not say when, or whether it would be a full payment, and he would send them word when the money arrived, they returned to their homes, but on the 14th of July came down again to the number of 5000 and camped. They said they were afraid they would not get their money, and had been again told so by the whites. Here they remained for sometime, all pinched for food and several dying from starvation. They dug up roots to appease their hunger and when corn was turned out to them, like animals, they devoured it uncooked.

Thus on the 17th day of August 1862, we find the instinctive hatred of this savage and ferocious people, who were able to bring into the field 1,300 well-armed warriors, the most expert and daring skirmishers in the world, fanned to a burning heat, by many years of actual and fancied wrong, and intensified by fears of hunger and cold. We find on the reservation the stores of the hated traders filled with goods which they have long sought to obtain and within easy access the unarmed people upon whom rage and mania for the feather way wreak itself in slaughter. On the 10th of August a party of twenty Indians from the Lower reservation went to the Big Woods near Forest City, to hunt deer. With the party was the chief, Makpeyahwetah. The hunt proving unsuccessful they separated, the chief and four others of the party going to a Mr. Whitcomb's.

The other fifteen going toward the town of Acton. On Sunday the 17th of August, when within six miles of that place, they got into a quarrel among themselves as to which of the party was the bravest. The dispute became so violent that the epithets of coward and squaw were freely used. The dispute waxed hotter and hotter as they proceeded on their way. The whole party became embroiled in it. Four of these were Upper Indians by birth, but had intermarried with the M'dewakantons, and were living with Shakopee's band at the mouth of Rice Creek. This band was the worst disposed on the reservation and most violent in its complaints against the whites. The others resided around the Lower Agency. The quarrel above related culminated in the murder of the Baker, Jones, and Webster families; and the shooting of Miss Clara D. Wilson of Acton. Such was the beginning of the Indian massacre of 1862. When the murderers had arrived at the agency and told their relatives what they had done, they determined at once to commit the massacre, knowing that unless they did so, the guilty parties would be caught and delivered up to justice. Little Crow, the principle chief of the Lower Agency being consulted at first opposed the project of the young men and the more reckless of the secret Indian lodge, who favored the extermination of the whites; but at last he was forced to yield to the clamor of the majority. The ties and affinities of kindred, the mad excitement of the hour, decided him and he said: "Trouble with the whites must come sooner or later. It may as well take place now as at any other time. I am with you. Let us go to the agency and kill the traders and take their goods." Then they sent word by swift runners to the bands of the Wabasha, Waconta and Red Legs; the Indians hastened with Crow to the agency, breaking up as they entered the village, into small parties, and surrounding the different houses and stores. It was agreed that the attack upon the houses and stores should be simultaneous and upon discharge of the first gun the massacre should commence. The doom of the people was sealed; the signal gun sounded, and suddenly as from the woods and the fields leaped upon them with the flashing of cataracts, death the crowned phantom, with all the equippage of his terrors and the tragic roar of his voice.

The first shot was fired at Myrick's store in the upper end of the town, between 6 and 7 o'clock in the morning. James Lynde was the first victim; then young Myrick was killed. At Forbes' store they killed Joe Balland and Antoin Young. At Robert's store, Brusson; and La Batte's, Mr. La Batte and his clerk. The superintendent of the farms was shot and the workmen in the brickyard. Many others perished at the same time. At Forbe's store they wounded George Spencer in the arms and side but he was saved by an Indian friend and was kept concealed by him in the Indian camp for several weeks or until after Sibley's command arrived at Camp Release.

While the Indians were plundering the stores, some escaped. Among them the Rev. Mr. Hindman who wrote a thrilling account of the scenes during the massacre.

Down the river, on each side below Fort Ridgley, and within six miles of New Ulm, and up the river to Yellow Medicine, the massacres that day extended. At Beaver Creek and at the Sacred Heart Creek, large numbers perished. Parties gathering for flight with their teams were overtaken and murdered. Quick and barbarous destruction was the portion of all the whites without distinction of age or sex. I cannot stop to give all the sickly details of that day of slaughter! Before noon the news of the outbreak reached the fort, and Capt. Marsh of the Fifth regiment started at once for the agency with forty-eight men. Marsh was advised by Mr. Hindman whom he met, not to attempt to cross the ferry, that the Indians outnumbered him ten to one; but he heeded not his council; in crossing, he was ambushed by the Indians

ANTELOPE BILL 125

concealed in the tall weeds near the river, and he and 24 of his men lost their lives.

During the day messengers were sent with the news to the upper Indians at Yellow Medicine. Upon reception of the same the Indians assembled in council to the number of 100 or more. They concluded to join the lower bands in their hellish work. They were opposed however, by John Other Day, a civilized Indian. By the efforts of this man and guided by him, a party of twenty men and forty-two women and children made their way to the settlements and were saved. He also sent word on Monday night at nine o'clock to the people at Mr. Rigg's place, six miles above the upper agency, and 42 including the missionaries, Riggs and Williamson, made their escape. Messengers were dispatched by the Indians at once to all their friends to notify them of what was being enacted. Fort Ridgley and New Ulm were filled with fugitives, that night, many bleeding from ghastly wounds and trembling from affright. Blazing houses were to be seen in every direction as the incendiaries plied the merciless torch. The frightened inmates prepared themselves for battle as well as they might, and dispatched messengers to the settlements for relief.

Little Crow, with three hundred warriors, left the agency for the fort during the morning pursuant to an understanding had the previous night; but on the way dissentions arose which resulted in a division of the force. One hundred and twenty under Little Crow went to the vicinity of the fort but made no attack that day. The remainder of the party, intent upon plunder, scattered themselves through the settlements around New Ulm and on the Cottonwood. At 4 o'clock a hundred of them gathered and made an attack on the town burning the buildings on the outskirts and killing several persons in the streets. This town then contained a population of 1,500 souls principally Germans; and this number was largely increased by the fugitives. On the next day Judge Flandreau reinforced New Ulm with a party from St. Peter. He found the people were in a state of utter frenzy with no organization for defense. The interior of the town was barricaded making a large square surrounded by wagons, barrels, and all kinds of trumpery, within which the people were huddled together like a flock of frightened sheep. At 1 o'clock P.M. on Wednesday the 20th of August, Little Crow being reinforced by those Indians who had been at New Ulm on the previous day, made an attack on Fort Ridgley and after hard fighting were repulsed with considerable loss to the savages, and with but slight loss to the garrison.

On Thursday morning the attack was renewed

and lasted about half an hour. In the evening of the same day the attack was again renewed and continued about the same length of time. Little Crow then returned to the agency for reinforcements, and after increasing his force to 450 men from the upper agency, whom he had sent for, he returned to the attack on the fort which he prosecuted with redoubled fury. The government stables were burned and some of the buildings in the fort were fired. Lieut. Sheehan gallantly and successfully held the fort and saved the lives of three hundred helpless women and children. My time precludes me from giving a more detailed account of the siege of Fort Ridgley. Early on Saturday morning, the 23d the Indians again made their way to New Ulm. Since Tuesday no attack had been made on that place and the time had been spent in strengthening their works, burying their dead, and scouting through the surrounding country. Many fugitives were thus rescued. At nine o'clock in the morning a series of fires were seen along the Fort Ridgley side of the river, commencing from the direction of the fort and rapidly nearing New Ulm.

The anxious inmates of the town knew that these arose from the burning houses along the road, and indicated the approach of their foes. As the fires reached opposite the town long lines of Indians were seen coming down the gullies, in the bluffs near the middle ferry and taking positions. A large force of Indians made their appearance two miles above the city. At a signal both parties made a simultaneous attack upon the town. Judge Flandreau believing a battle on the open prairie would be more advantageous to the whites, posted all his available force, some 250 men, aided by the citizens, on the open field outside the town. The Indians advanced to the attack and a terrific battle ensued, continuing for five hours with varying results on each side. The Indians taking advantage of a strong wind which was blowing towards the town, and protected by the smoke of the burning buildings which they had fired as they advanced, were enabled to destroy the entire city, save the small portion enclosed within the barricade. At last the savages were repulsed, after the town was laid in ashes. Then the people of New Ulm fearing they might be attacked again by a still larger force, abandoned their town and went to Mankato 2,000 in number, carrying their sick and wounded in a train of 253 wagons.

While New Ulm and Fort Ridgley were attacked, the depredations extended throughout the whole western frontier of Minnesota and into Iowa and Dakota. During that week over 1,200 people perished and about 200 people were made captives. On Tuesday two Indians killed Mr. Amos Huggins, at Lac-qui-parle. On Wednesday they began murdering at Lake Shetek, and Spirit Lake in Iowa, and also in the neighborhood of Forest City, 120 miles apart. Most of my readers have read of the escape of Mrs. Hurd from Lake Shetek and reaching New Ulm a distance of 90 miles, carrying two children, one an infant and subsisting during the journey on berries and green corn, and of the hardships endured by Mrs. Estlick and her children. A recital of all the atrocious barbarities, perpetrated on the defenceless settlers on the frontier of Minnesota during the terrible week of terror and death, would be too revolting to give in public discourse.

We will therefore return to Col. Sibley, whom we left at St. Peter making preparations for an advance movement. On Sunday his force was increased by the arrival of some 200 mounted men called the Cullen guard under command of W. J. Cullen. These with about 100 more mounted men were placed under command of Col. Samuel McPhail. On the same day six more companies of the Sixth regiment under Col. Crooks. Several companies of volunteer militia had also congregated here, which swelled Sibley's command to some 1,400 men. St. Peter, where he now was, a large straggling town of several thousand inhabitants and increased to double its true number, presented a picture of excitement not easily forgotten. Oxen were killed in the streets and the meat hastily prepared, cooked over fires made on the ground. All thought of property was abandoned. Safety of life prevailed over every other consideration. Many of the wounded and mutilated were brought in from the surrounding country, who subsequently died, after lingering many days in agony. On the 26th Lieut. Gov. Donnelly wrote to the executive from St. Peter: "You can hardly conceive the panic existing along this valley. In Belle Plain I found 600 people crowded. In this place the leading citizens assure me there are between three and four thousand refugees. On the road to New Ulm and Mankato are over two thousand. Mankato also is crowded. The people here are in a state of panic. They fear to see our forces leave. The people will continue to pour down the valley carrying consternation wherever they go, their property in the meantime abandoned and going to ruin.

The safety of these towns and the panic-stricken people depended entirely upon Col. Sibley's success, and he could not risk everything to march until prepared.

On Thursday August 25th Col. Sibley left St. Peter with his command for Fort Ridgely where he arrived on the 28th; during this march several dead bodies were discovered and buried. A Mr. Richardson from Glencoe who volunteered to go to Fort Ridgley and ascertain the news in reference to progress of the Indian war was murdered near the fort. His body was found by Co. F and buried on the spot where found. It was subsequently removed to Glencoe. Intrenchments were thrown up around the fort and upon a neighboring elevation which commanded the camp. Cannon were placed in position and a strong guard continually kept up. The first two nights after the arrival of the forces, shots were fired into the camp, and a general attack expected; but none came. It could never be satisfactorily determined whether the shots were from Indians or were ordered by the commander for the purpose of trying the raw troops to see if they were prepared for a night attack!

On the 1st day of September Lieut. Col. Marshall with a portion of the Seventh regiment joined the expedition. All that was now needed for a forward movement was ammunition and provisions; but these did not arrive in sufficient quantity for many days afterward. Excitement soon came in most woeful shape.

BIRCH COOLIE

On Sunday, the last day of August, Capt. Grant's army of infantry, seventy men of the Cullen guard under Capt. Anderson, and a detail of citizens and soldiers from other companies of the Sixth regiment together with seventeen teamsters with teams, numbering in all about 150 men were dispatched under command of Major Joe Brown to the lower agency for the purpose of burying the dead and ascertain if possible the whereabouts of the enemy. The next morning the cavalry and a small portion of the infantry crossed the river at the agency, buried the dead, and went some little distance above and found no indications of the Indians having been there for several days. Capt. Grant with the Infantry, interred the dead on the Fort Ridgley side including those at Beaver Creek and camped during the afternoon on the same side of the river, where they were joined in the evening by Major Brown and his detachment. Brown seeing no signs of Indians about the agency led him to believe there were none in the vicinity. The place was selected for camping because of its proximity to wood and water; but as subsequent events showed, a worse site could not have been selected in the state! It was within gunshot of the head of the wooded ravine on one side and of an elevation on the other, from behind which, an attacking party could command the camp with safety to themselves.

Major Brown was correct however in his conclusion that the Indians had left the lower agency several days before. On Thursday four days after the last attack on New Ulm, hearing of Sibley's march to the fort and anxious to place their families in safety, they had moved up above the Yellow Medicine river. Shortly after, an Indian who had been getting his traps back of New Ulm, told them that he had been within view of the town and that it appeared to him to be deserted. On hearing this a war party was at once organized to proceed to New Ulm and get what plunder they wanted and then attack St. Peter and Mankato.

Early Monday morning 349 warriors with a long train of wagons to carry their plunder, started down the river on the reservation side under Gray Bird of Little Crow's band. One hundred and ten more under Crow, followed in an hour with the intention of joining them but crossed the river at Yellow Medicine to meet any troops which might be coming up on that side to attack their families. They changed their minds after they had marched five or six miles and went towards the Big Woods in the neighborhood of Acton.

When Gray Bird's force arrived at the Lower

Agency they caught sight of Major Brown's horsemen winding up the ravine to Grant's camp. Runners were sent over to watch them and ascertain if they were moving towards Yellow Medicine or the fort. When these returned and informed them that the whites had encamped their joy knew no bounds and they at once resolved on the attack which followed. During the night the Indians quietly crossed the river and marched up the ravine whose high banks concealed them. Before daylight they were within short musket range of Brown's camp, the occupants of which were sleeping soundly after the previous day's fatigue, unconscious of the terrific volcano that was about to burst upon them. Between the Sibley tents and the wooded banks of the ravine which was not more than ten rods distant, there was stretched on picket pins a large rope in the form of an elipse. To this rope there were tied by their halters, ninety cavalry horses. The wagons were between the tents and the horses. Just as it began to dawn gray in the east, one of the sentinels thought he saw something creeping towards him in the grass. He fired at it and before the echoes of the report died away a volley from three hundred guns within a hundred yards of the slumbering camp, raked the tents "fore and aft." For more than three hours this firing was kept up with scarcely an intermission and in that fatal three hours some twenty men were killed or mortally wounded, and some sixty severely wounded and ninety horses killed. After the effects of the first fire was partially over, the men commenced to dig, and dig they did, with one pick, three spades, a couple of old axes, knives, bayonets, tin plates, and sticks, and by four o'clock p.m., they had holes enough in the ground to protect them from shooting at a distance. When they were relieved by Col. Sibley they had been thirty-one hours without food or water, with but thirty rounds of ammunition to a man when they commenced, and less than five when relieved. This was the severest battle of the war in proportion to the number engaged. One horse alone survived and he was terribly wounded. Capt. Grant had found a woman the day before near Beaver Creek, who though severely wounded by a charge of buckshot, had made her escape from the massacre near Patterson's Rapids. She had been fourteen days without seeing a human being, and had eaten nothing during this time but a few berries obtained by dragging herself through the briers. When found she was nearly dead, and in such an exhausted state as to be almost unable to speak and could give but little account of herself or her sufferings. She was lying in a high wagon in the center of the camp during the attack, and strange as it may seem, she received no injury though a number of balls passed through the wagon from different directions and the spokes of the wheels were cut to pieces by the bullets. God would not break the bruised reed.

While the battle of Birch Coolie was going on, the sentries at Fort Ridgley eighteen miles away, as they walked their beats, heard the volleys of musketry distinctly. When this was reported in camp, the eminences were surrounded quickly with anxious listeners. The wind was blowing strongly towards the direction from which the sound was stated to have proceeded, but by throwing one's self upon the ground the rapid discharge of firearms could be easily heard. Col. McPhail with fifty horsemen, Maj. McLaren with 105 Infantry, Lieut. Sheehan with a few men, and Capt. Mark Hendricks with a mountain Howitzer, were at once ordered to their relief. The writer will here mention that Lieut. Sheehan was ordered back to Fort Ridgley for reinforcements, running the Indian gauntlet, his horse being shot twice and not being injured himself.

Col. Sibley started with his whole command accompanied by Sergeant Jones with two pieces of cannon. A slow weary march of fifteen miles amid the darkness, which was now intense, was lit up by a bright flash, followed by the quick roar of the howitzer, and guided by its repeated discharges to which our cannons answered we found ourselves at the camp of the second detachment. We then threw ourselves down on the grass and waited for the daylight. At early dawn the entire force was in motion. As we neared Birch Coolie tents could be seen through the trees and speculations were as to whether it was Brown's camp or that of the Indians as they have tents very similar to our own. The Indians were soon seen swarming through a belt of woods toward our marching column from the direction of the tents, and quickly scattering along the line, waving their blankets and shouting defiance. Some were mounted, and one on a white horse was conspicuous, riding up and down the line and encouraging his comrades. As they approached nearer to us they threw themselves down behind eminences which would afford protection, and poured a rapid fire into our column. Nearly all the bullets flew too high, or were spent and only one of our men was wounded. Skirmishers were at once thrown out, who, with quick discharges drove them back, and the bursting shells from the cannon soon put them to flight. They retreated rapidly down Birch Coolie and crossed the river at the agency. When we reached Brown's camp the scene presented was most horrible and one the soldiers can never forget.

The camp was surrounded by the dead bodies of the horses, ninety in number, perforated with bullets. The tents were riddled with balls as many as 104 being found to have passed through a single one. Ditches were dug between the tents and the horses and the dirt piled on them so as to form a breastwork. Within this circuit lay 16 of the soldiers dead, and a number mortally wounded, and a few feet distant were more dead bodies. The groanings of the wounded could be heard a long distance off. William Irvine, of West St. Paul, presented a terrible spectacle. He had been shot in the head and his brains were oozing over his face; and yet he lived for a number of hours, his breathing heavily and painfully distinct. After the dead were buried the command returned to the fort carrying the wounded with them.

Col. Sibley was compelled to remain many days inactive at Fort Ridgley for want of ammunition and supplies; the time was improved by the troops, by daily drills. Col. Sibley was carrying on a correspondence during this time with the Indians in reference to the relief of the white captives held by them. These consisted of about 250 in number nearly all of whom were women. At the time, I thought Col. Sibley was inexcusably dillatory in advancing towards the Indians; but since examining the matter more thoroughly, I am satisfied he pursued the wisest course. I have talked freely with him in regard to the motives that actuated him in his dealing with Indians during that fall, and I am perfectly certain that from his knowledge of Indian character, gained by many years' residence among them, he was the very best man in the state that could have been selected to conduct that campaign. Had he marched at once against their camp, the prisoners would probably all have been massacred. Many of the Indians favored this course, but by delay and negotiations with such of the chiefs as were known to be friendly, to the whites and who were opposed to the war, their lives were saved. On the 18th of September the camp at Fort Ridgley was broken up, and the expedition disgusted with long inactivity, joyfully started on its upward march after the foe. The river was crossed opposite the fort. The first night we camped at Four Mile Lake; the second near the Redwood agency. None of the enemy were seen during these two days.

Early the third morning we proceeded on our way. On passing a new grave we found several hundred little sticks thrust into the fresh dirt indicating the number of Indians who had visited it. They were scouts from the camp above Yellow Medicine. As we advanced we could see these scouts on their ponies on every hillock, watching our movements until we came near, then they would scud away. They amused themselves by firing several bridges to impede our progress. These were smoking when we came up, but not materially injured. The next day George Gleason's body was found on the prairie and buried. He was Mr. Galbraith's clerk at the Lower agency and well known throughout the state. On the evening of the 22d we camped on the Lone-Tree Lake, two miles from Wood Lake and two from the Yellow Medicine river. Next morning between six and seven o'clock, as we were taking our breakfast some foraging teams with their guards when about half a mile from camp were fired upon by Indians who laid concealed in the grass. The guards returned the fire while the teams were turned about and urged to their utmost speed. The Third regiment under Major Welch which had joined us at the fort hurried out without orders from the commander of the expedition, crossed a ravine and was soon engaged with the foe. The Third were ordered back into camp and just then the enemy appeared in great numbers on all sides and were gathering in the ravine between the regiment and the camp. In justice to the Third Minnesota regiment, I desire to say that although they were accused by many of acting in a very lawless manner and disregarding necessary military discipline, while on this campaign, there are many things that can be offered by way of excuse for them. It will be remembered that the Third regiment had been surrendered to the rebels at Murfreesborough, Tenn., through the cowardice of its colonel and a majority of its officers. The men were paroled and permitted to return to their homes while waiting to be exchanged, while their officers were held as prisoners of war in the South. The Third was as fine and brave a regiment of soldiers as left Minnesota during the rebellion; but at this time they were without officers; they did not know whether or not they had been, or would be exchanged; they felt desperate, reckless and ugly. They enlisted to fight and not to be surrendered to the enemy; and smarting under a sense of apparent disgrace, they seemed to care but little what they did. Hence they were more than glad of an opportunity to fight the Indians, though the latter outnumbered them ten to one. With this intense desire to fight they were now accommodated and although surrounded by many times their number, and many of them badly wounded including the brave Maj. Welch, and several killed, they cut their way out carrying their wounded comrades with them. The battle which was known as that of Wood Lake had now fairly begun. The bullets flew thick and fast some of them penetrating the tents. The cannons now opened fire as did the howitzers.

Col. Marshall with three companies of the Seventh and Capt. Grant of the Sixth, charged amid a shower of balls, on the double quick, through the ravine and put the Indians to rout. While the Seventh regiment were engaged on the east side of the lake with the main body of Indians another detachment of them came around the west end following a ravine which was concealed by an intervening ridge and attempted to get into the rear of our encampment. Co. F was detached and ordered forward to intercept them. The company started out on the double quick, and met the Indians before they had time to gain the elevation of the ridge; and after considerable sharp fighting, they were repulsed and retreated rapidly over the opposite ridge towards the Yellow Medicine river. During this attack the captain of Company F. was wounded. The contest lasted about an hour and a half. The number actually engaged on each side was about 800, many of our men being held in camp as a reserve. Our loss was four killed and about 50 wounded, among whom were several Red Wing boys; Ben Densmore and Hermen Pettibone were among them. Maj. Welch was very severely wounded having the bones of one of his legs shattered. At the conclusion of the battle the Indians requested leave to carry away their dead but were refused. Fifteen Indians were found dead upon the battle field and buried and a wounded one brought in as a prisoner. He lived three days although shot through the lungs, protesting all the while that he was a good Indian. After remaining one day at Wood lake we marched to the Indian camp near Lac-qui-Parle.

The writer gives great credit to the Renville Rangers for their daring deeds at these battles as each one wears his medal as a token of bravery and among them H. Peirce, the writer's brother.

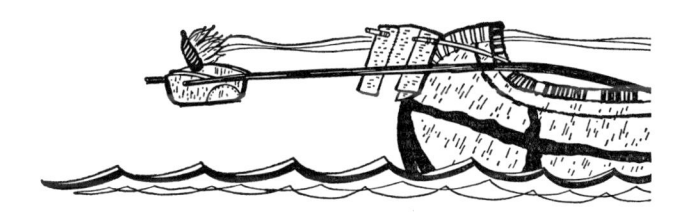

We reached there on the 26th of September. It was located nearly opposite the mouth of the Chippewa river and about four miles from where Montevideo is now located, and numbered about 100 tepees. Little Crow and some 200 men and their families rapidly fled the day after the battle. Our own camp which was called Camp Release, was pitched about a quarter of a mile from that of the Indians which our cannon commanded. Their camp was filled with wagons and cattle which they had stolen. Their tents were well supplied with carpets and different kinds of goods and household utensils which they had taken from the houses of our murdered citizens. Soon after our arrival the commander rode over and took possession and posted a strong guard around it to prevent the escape of any of the inmates. A formal demand which was made for the captives was instantly complied with. They were nearly 250 in number. They had been compelled to wear the Indian dress during their captivity but had now been permitted to resume their former habiliments. The poor creatures wept for joy at their escape. They had watched for our coming for many a weary day. The woe written in the faces of the half-starved and nearly naked women and children would have melted the hardest heart. They were taken to our camp where they remained until sent below a few days afterwards. On the 1st day of October at Camp Release the Sixth regiment was mustered into the service of the United States, having left Fort Snelling in such haste as to prevent this ceremony's being performed. A military commission of inquiry was at once appointed to ascertain the guilty parties, and testimony against about a dozen obtained. A commission for the trial of these, and of any others who might be accused was then organized and some thirty or forty were arrested. The remainder in camp were sent down to the Yellow Medicine, under the charge of Agent Galbraith, as the stock of provisions was fast becoming exhausted.

The prisoners were linked together in pairs, by chains forged to their ankles. On the 23d of

October the tents were struck, and with the Indian prisoners in wagons, we commenced our homeward march. At Yellow Medicine we took in the other prisoners and that night we pitched our tents in the valley of the Redwood. The Indian camp, consisting principally of women and children had been previously removed to this place from Yellow Medicine. It was soon after moved to Ft. Snelling under the command of Col. Marshall. Several weeks were spent at the lower agency, the trials still progressing. During the time the Sixth and Seventh regiments were daily exercised in the evolutions of the battalion drill. Here was the most comfortable camping ground we had found during the campaign.

The male prisoners had been confined in the jail which had been constructed and the trials were held in a log building attached to La Batte's store. Over three hundred Indians were found guilty, and condemned to be hung, but President Lincoln pardoned all but thirty-eight of them. On the 7th of November Sibley moved to the vicinity of Mankato going into camp on a flat at the junction of the Minnesota and Blue Earth rivers, a log jail having been built there for the reception of the prisoners. They were subsequently removed into the city of Mankato where they were confined in a stone building on Main street nearly opposite the end of the present bridge across the Minnesota river. When the command passed through New Ulm, the inhabitants hearing we were coming with the Indian prisoners, rushed forth, men, women and children armed with clubs, pitchforks, hoes, brickbats, knives, spades and guns, and attacked the prisoners. The women were perfectly furious, they danced around with their aprons full of stones, and cried for an opportunity to get at the Indians, upon whom they poured the most violent abuse. Many rushed forward and discharged a shower of stones. The writer remembers most vividly one woman who passed near him as his company was marching on either side of the wagon containing the prisoners with loaded muskets and fixed bayonets to guard them against the fury of the people of New Ulm; she had a long knife in her hand; her eyes flashed with the ferociousness of a fiend and the only thing that restrained her from breaking through our lines, was the gleam of a bayonet presented to her breast. Another, somehow, got through and pounded an Indian in the face till she broke his jaw, and he fell backward out of his wagon and died a few days afterwards from his injuries. It must be remembered that these were the brutal murderers of their friends. The expedition soon reached Camp Lincoln as it was called above Mankato.

Execution of 38 Sioux Indians
at Mankato, Minn.

On Monday afternoon Col. Miller addressed the prisoners as follows:

"The commanding officer of this place has called to speak to you on a very serious subject this afternoon. Your Great Father at Washington after carefully reading what your witnesses have testified in your several trials have come to the conclusion that you have each been guilty of wickedly and wantonly murdering his white children; and for this reason he has directed that you each be hanged by the neck until you are dead on next Friday, and that order will be carried into effect that day at 10 o'clock in the forenoon.

Good ministers, both Catholic and Protestant are here from among whom each of you can select your spiritual adviser, who will be permitted to commune constantly with you during the four days you are yet to live."

The colonel then instructed Adjt. Arnold to read to them in English the letter of President Lincoln which in substance ordered that 38 prisoners whose names are given, shall be executed at the time above stated. Rev. Mr. Riggs then read the letter in the Dakota language. The colonel further instructed Mr. Riggs to tell them that they had sinned so against their fellow man that there is no hope for clemency except in the mercy of God, through the merits of the Blessed Redeemer, and that he earnestly exhorted them to apply to that as their only remaining source of consolation.

The occasion was one of much solemnity to the persons present, though but very little emotion was manifested by the Indians. A half-breed named Millord seemed much depressed in spirits. All listened attentively and at the conclusion of each sentence indulged in their usual grunt or signal of approval. At the reading of that portion of the warrant condemning them to be hanged by the necks, the response was quite feeble and was given by only two or three. Several Indians smoked their pipes composedly during the reading, and we observed one in particular, who, when the time of execution was designated, quietly knocked the ashes from his pipe and filled it afresh with his favorite kinnekinnick; while another was slowly rubbing a pipe full of the same article in his hand preparatory to a good smoke. The Indians were evidently prepared for the visit and the announcement of their sentence—one or two having overheard soldiers talking about it, when they were removed to a separate apartment.

At the conclusion of the ceremony Col. Miller instructed Maj. Brown to tell the Indians that each would be privileged to designate the minister of his choice, that a record of the same would be made and the minister so selected have free intercourse with him. The colonel and spectators then withdrew, leaving the ministers in consultation with the prisoners.

The Indians under sentence were confined in a back room on the first floor of Leech's stone building chained in pairs and strongly guarded.

The following are the Indian names of the condemned prisoners:

1. Te-he-do-ne-cha (One who forbids his house), says he was sleeping when the outbreak took place at the Lower agency. He was not present at the breaking open of the stores, but afterwards went over the Minnesota river and took some women captives. The men who were killed there he says were killed by other Indians, whom he named.

2. Ptan-doo-ta, alias Ta-joo (Red Otter), says he had very sore eyes at the time of the outbreak, and was at that time down opposite Fort Ridgley. He was with the party that killed Patwell. Ma-ya-bon-doo killed Patwell. He took Miss Williams captive. Says he would have violated the women but they resisted. He thinks he done a good deed in saving the women alive.

3. Wy-a-tah-ta-wa (His people) says he was at the attack on Cap. Marsh's Company, and also at New Ulm. He and another Indian shot a man at the same time. He does not know whether he or the other Indian killed the white man.

He was wounded in following up another white man. He was at the battle of Birch Coolie where he fired his gun four times; he fired twice at Wood Lake.

4. Hin-han-shoon-ko-yag-ma-ne (One who walks clothed in an owl's tail), says he is

charged with killing white people, and so condemned; he does not know certainly that he killed any one; he was in all the battles. That is all he has to say.

5. Ma-za-boom-doo (Iron Blower), says he was down on the Big Cottonwood when the outbreak took place; that he came that day into New Ulm and purchased various articles and then started home; he met the Indians coming down; saw some in wagons shot but does not know who killed them; he was present at the killing of Patwell and others, but denies having done it himself; he thinks he done well by Mattie Williams and Mary Swan, in keeping them from being killed; they now live and he has to die, which he thinks not quite fair.

6. Wa-pa-doo-ta (Red Leaf), is an old man; he says he was mowing when he heard of the outbreak; he saw some men after they were killed about the agency, but did not kill any one there; he started down to the Fort and went on to the New Ulm settlement; there he shot at a man through a window, but does not think he killed him; he was himself wounded at New Ulm.

7. Wa-he-hua (do not know what his name means), says he did not kill any one; if he had believed he had killed a white man he would have fled with Little Crow; the witnesses lied on him.

8. Qua-ma-ne (Tinkling Walker) says he was condemned on the testimony of two German boys; they say he killed two persons; the boys lied. He was not at that place at all.

9. Ta-tah-me-ma (Round Wind) is a brother-in-law of the former well known Mr. Joseph Renville; he was the public crier for Little Crow before and during the outbreak; after the battle at Wood Lake he came over to the opposition, and was the crier at Camp Release when the captives were delivered up; he was condemned on the testimony of two German boys who said they saw him kill their mother; the old man denies the charge and says he was not across the river at that time, and that he was unjustly condemned. He is the only one of the 38 who has been at all in the habit of attending Protestant worship; Last Sabbath he requested Dr. Williamson to baptize him, professing repentance and faith in Jesus Christ; which was done on Monday before he knew he was among those to be hung at this time. May God have mercy on his soul.

10. Rda-in-you-ka (Rattling Runner), says he did not know of the uprising on Monday, the 18th August until they had killed a number of men; he went out and met Little Crow and tried to stop the murders but could not. The next day his son was brought home wounded from

Fort Ridgley. He forbade the delivery of the white captives to Paul when he demanded them, and he supposes he is to be hung for that.

11. Do-wan-sa (The Singer) says he was one of the six who were down in the Swan Lake neighborhood; he knows they killed two men and two women, but this was done by the rest of the party and not by himself.

12. Ha-pan (second child, if a son) says he was not in the massacre of New Ulm, nor the agency; he was with the company who killed Patwell and his companions, he took one of the women. O-va-tay-ta-wa killed Patwell.

13. Shoon-ka-ska (white dog) says that when the outbreak took place he ran away and did not get any of the stolen property; at the ferry he talked with Quinn; first called to them to come over, but when he saw the Indians were in ambush, he beckoned to Capt. Marsh to stay back, he says his position and conduct at the ferry were misunderstood and misrepresented, that he wanted peace and did not commend the Indians to fire on Capt. Marsh's men; that another man should be put to death for that, and complains bitterly that he did not have a chance to tell things as they were; that he could not have an opportunity of refuting the false testimony brought against him; he says they all expected to have another trial—that they were

promised it; that they have done great wrong to the white people and do not refuse to die, but they think it hard that they should not have a fairer trial. They want the president to know this.

14. Toon-kan-e-chah-tag-ma-ne (o n e who walks by his grandfather), says he took nothing from the stores except a blanket; he was at Ft. Ridgley, but killed nobody. He is charged with killing white persons in a wagon, but he did not; they were killed by another man.

15. E-tag-doo-ta (Red Face), says he was woke up in the morning of Monday the 18th of August, but did not kill any one.

16. Am-da-cha (broken to pieces) says he was doctoring a girl when he learned of the outbreak at the Lower agency; he went with others and took some things from Mr. Forbe's store; he fired his gun only twice but thinks he did not kill any one.

17. Hay-pe-dan (the third child if a son), says he was not at the stores until all was over there; he was with Wabasha and with him opposed the outbreak. He was afterwards driven into it by being called a coward. He went across the Minnesota river and took two horses, and afterward captured a woman and two children. He tried to keep a white man from being killed,

but could not. He was at the ferry when Marsh's men were killed but had only a bow and arrows there. He was in three battles and shot six times but he does not know that he killed any one.

18. Mah-pe-o-ke-ne-jin (who stands on the cloud), Cut-nose says that when Little Crow proposed to kill the traders he went along; he says he is charged with having killed a carpenter, but he did not do it; he fired off his gun in one of the stores; his nephew was killed at Ft. Ridgley; he was out at Hutchinson when his son was killed. Little Crow took them out. He was hungry and went over to an ox, and when there saved Mr. Brown's family.

19. Henry Millord, a half-breed. Henry says he went over the Minnesota river with Baptiste Campbell, and others; they were forced to go by Little Crow. He fired his gun at a woman but does not think he killed her, several others fired at her also. He did not see her afterwards. Henry Millord was raised by Gen. Sibley. He was a smart active intelligent young man, and as such, would be likely to be drawn into the Dakota rebellion; indeed, it was next to impossible for young men whether halfbreeds or full-bloods to keep out of it. They are to be pitied as well as blamed.

20. Chas-kay-dan (the first born if a son) says

he went to the stores in the morning of Monday; then he saw Little Crow taking away goods. He then went up to Redwood with a relation of his and were told that a white man was coming on the road; they went out to meet him but the first who came along was a half-breed. They let him pass. Then came along Mr. Gleason and Mrs. Wakefield: his friend shot Mr. Gleason and he attempted to fire on him but his gun did not go off. He saved Mrs. Wakefield and the children, and now he dies while she lives.

21. Baptiste Campbell is the son of Scott Campbell, who was for many years United States interpreter at Fort Snelling, thinks they ought to have had a new trial; says he did not speak advisedly when before the military commission. He went over the Minnesota river with four others. They were sent over by Little Crow and told to get all the cattle they could and kill every white man—if they did not the Soldier's Lodge would take care of them; they went over to a farm between Beaver Creek and Birch Coolie, where they found a lot of cattle which they attempted to drive. The cattle however, ran away and their attention was attracted to the owner. Campbell fired his gun first but did not hit the man. He says his statement before the commission was misunderstood. Said he was a good shot and if he had fired at the

man he would have killed him. He fired over him intentionally and fired because he felt compelled to do so by command of Little Crow. Campbell says that Little Crow compelled him and his brother Joseph to go out to Hutchinson. They tried to get away at the time of the attack on Capt. Strout's company but were prevented; they were forced to go to the battle of Hutchinson. Little Crow told them if they did not kill the white men they would be killed, but he did not shoot any men there.

22. Ta-ta-ka-gay (Wind Maker) was quite a young man—a grandson of Sacret Walker, who took care of Mrs. Josephine Higgins and her children in their captivity; was one of those who killed Amos W. Higgins at Lac-qui-Parle. The other two who are probably the most guilty have escaped; says he was at Red Iron's village when he heard of the outbreak. Another Indian urged him to go up with him and kill Mr. Higgins. He refused at first, but afterwards went. His comrade shot Mr. Higgins and killed him; he then fired off his gun but held it up.

23. Hay-pin-kpa (the tip of the horn) is condemned because he boasted of having shot Stewart B. Garvie with an arrow. As it is not known that Mr. Garvie was shot with an arrow, but with buckshot, it is probably true, as he said before the commission that he lied about it.

This is not the first time a man has been killed for lying. He now says that they determined to send all the white people from the Yellow Medicine without killing any. Mr. Garvie refused to go; he did not shoot him. He dies without being guilty of the charge and he trusts in the Great Spirit to save him in the other world.

24. Hypolite Ange was a half-breed; says he had been a clerk in one of the stores previous to the outbreak; was sent down the Minnesota river with Baptiste Campbell and others, by Little Crow; shot the white man but not until after he had been killed by others.

25. Na-pa-shue (One who does not flee) says that at the time of the outbreak he was quite lame—that he was not engaged in any of the massacres; he was not engaged in any battle but was forced with others to come down to Yellow Medicine before the battle of Wood Lake; he dies for no fault of his.

26. Wa-kan-tau-ka (Great Spirit) says he was not present at the commencement of the outbreak; was along with the company that came down from New Ulm; saw the men in two wagons killed but he did not kill any one; says one witness before the commission testified that he killed one of those men, but the witness lied on him.

27. Toon kan-ko-yag-e-na-jin (one who stands clothed with his grandfather) says that he was in the battle of Hutchinson, but does not know that he killed any one.

28. Ma-ka-ta-e-na jin (one who stands on the earth) is an old man; says he has not used a gun for years; was down at New Ulm but did not kill any one; had two sons killed; wants to have the truth told.

29. Pa-za-koo-tag-ma-ne (one who walks prepared to shoot) says he was one in a war party against the Chippewas when the outbreak took place; when he came back the massacres were over; he did not kill any one. Says his statement before the commission was not understood. When he was asked whether he was in a war party and fired his gun, he replied; "yes, but it was against the Chippewas, and not against the whites."

30. Ta-ta-hde-dan (wind comes home) said that the men of Rice Creek were the authors of the outbreak; tried to keep them from killing white people but only succeeded partially.

31. Wa-she-choon (Frenchman) says he did not know anything about killing white people; is to die for no crime. Was very much affected.

32. A-e-cha-ga (to grow upon) is charged with participating in the murder of an old man and two girls; and makes no confession nor denial.

33. Ko tan-in-koo (voice that appears coming), says he did not have a gun; was at the Big Woods and struck a man with his hatchet after he had been shot by another man. Did not abuse any white woman.

34. Chay-tan-hoon-ka (the parent hawk) says he killed no one; was down at Fort Ridgley and also at Beaver Creek and took horses from there but did not kill the man.

35. Chan-ka-hda (near the woods) says he took Mary Anderson captive after she had been shot by another man and thinks it rather hard he is to be hung for another's crime.

36. Hda-hin-day (to make a rattling noise suddenly) says he was up north at the time of the outbreak and did not come down until after the killing of the whites was passed; was at the battle of Wood lake; says he is charged with having killed two children but the charge is false.

37. O-ya-tag-a-kso (the coming people) says he was with the company that killed Patwell and others; he is charged with striking him with a hatchet after he was shot. This charge he denies.

38. Ma-hoo-way-ma (he comes for me) says he was out in one of the raids towards the Big Woods; did not kill anybody but he struck a

woman who had been killed before; was himself wounded.

And now, guilty or not guilty, may God have mercy upon these 38 poor human creatures, and if it be possible save them in the other world through Jesus Christ His Son. Amen.

In making these statements, confessions and denials, they were generally calm but a few individuals were quite excited. They were immediately checked by others and told that they were all dead men and there was no reason why they should not all tell the truth. Many of them have indicted letters to their friends, in which they are very dear to them but will see them no more. They exhort them not to cry nor to change their dress for them. Some of them say they expect to go and dwell with the Good Spirit and express the hope that their friends will all join them there.

On Tuesday evening they extemporized a dance with a wild Indian song. It was feared that this was only a cover for something else which might be attempted and their chains were thereafter fastened to the floor. It seems however, rather probable, that they were only singing their death song. Their friends from the other prison have been in to bid them farewell and they are now ready to die.

The following is a copy of a letter from one of

the condemned prisoners to his chief and father-in-law, Wabasha. It was taken down in the exact language dictated by the prisoner, and excepting its untruthfulness, we think it an excellent letter.

"Wabasha: You have deceived me. You told me that if we followed the advice of Gen. Sibley and give ourselves up to the whites all would be well—no innocent man would be injured. I have not killed, injured or wounded a white man or any white persons. I have not participated in the plunder of their property; and yet to day I am set apart for execution and must die in a few days while men who are guilty will remain in prison. My wife is your daughter, my children are your grandchildren. I leave them all in your care and under your protection. Do not let them suffer, and when my children are grown up let them know that their father died because he followed the advice of his chief, and without having the blood of a white man to answer for to the Great Spirit. My wife and children are dear to me. Let them not grieve for me. Let them remember that the brave should be prepared to meet death and I will do so as becomes a Dacotah."

Your son-in-law,
Rda-in-you-ka.

The above Indian was convicted of participating in the murders and robberies at the Upper Agency and the sworn testimony at Washington differs materially from his confession as given above.

An Effecting Scene

On Wednesday, each Indian set apart for execution, was permitted to send for two or three of his relatives or friends, confined in the main prison for the purpose of bidding them a final adieu and to carry such messsages to the absent relatives as each person might be disposed to send. Major Brown was present at the interview; and describes it as very sad and affecting. Each Indian had some word to send his parents or family. When speaking of their wives and children, almost every one was affected to tears.

Good counsel was sent to the children. They were in many cases exhorted to an adoption of Christianity and a life of good feeling toward the whites. Most of them spoke confidently of their hopes of salvation. They had been constantly attended by Rev. Dr. Williamson, Rev. Ravoux and Rev. S. R. Riggs whose efforts in bringing these poor criminals to the knowledge of the merits of the Blessed Redeemer had been eminently successful. These gentlemen were all conversant with the Dakotah language, and could converse and plead with the Indians in their own language.

Fun is a ruling passion with many Indians and even Ta-zoo could not refrain from it in this sad hour. Ta-ti-mi-ma was sending word to his relatives not to mourn his loss. He said he was old and could not hope to live long under any circumstances, and his execution would not shorten his days a great deal, and dying as he did innocent of any white man's blood, he hoped would give him a better chance to be saved. Therefore he hoped his friends would consider his death but as a removal from this to a better world. I have every hope said he of going to the abode of the Great Spirit, where I shall always be happy. This latter remark reached the ears of Ta-zoo, who was also speaking to his friends and he elaborated on it in this wise: "Yes, tell our friends that we are being removed from this world over the same path they must shortly travel. We go first but many of our friends may follow us in a very short time. I expect to go direct to the abode of the Great Spirit and be happy when I get there; but we are told that the road is long and the distance great, therefore as I am slow in all my movements it will probably take me a long time to reach the end of my journey and I should not be surprised if some of the young active men we will leave behind us will pass me on the road before I reach the place of my destination."

In shaking hands with Red Iron and Akipa

ANTELOPE BILL 167

Ta-zoo said: "Friends, last summer you were opposed to us. You were living in continual apprehension of an attack from those who determined to exterminate the whites. Yourselves and families were subject to many taunts, insults and threats. Still you stood firm in your friendship for the whites and continually counselled the Indians to abandon their raid against the whites. Your course was condemned at the time but now we see your wisdom. You were right when you said the whites could not be exterminated and the attempt indicated folly. You and your families were prisoners, and the lives of all in constant danger. To-day you are here at liberty assisting in feeding and guarding us and 38 men will die in two days because they did not follow your example and advice."

Several of the prisoners were completely overcome during the leave taking, and were compelled to abandon conversation. Others again, and Ta-zoo was one, affected to disregard the danger, and joked apparently as unconcerned as if they were sitting around a camp fire in their perfect freedom.

On Thursday, the women who were employed as cooks for the prisoners, all of whom had relations among the condemned, were admitted to the prison. This interview was less sad but was still interesting. Locks of hair, blankets, coats, and almost every other article in the possession of the prisoners, were given in trust for some relative or friend who had been forgotten or overlooked during the interview of the previous day. At this interview far less feeling was displayed than at the interview of Wednesday. The idea of allowing women to witness their weakness is repugnant to an Indian and will account for this. The messages sent were principally advice to their friends to bear themselves with fortitude and refrain from great mourning. The confidence of many in their salvation was again reiterated.

On Thursday evening we paid a brief visit to the condemned prisoners in their cell. The Catholic ministers were baptizing a number of them. All the prisoners seemed resigned to the fate and much depressed in spirits. Many sat perfectly motionless and more like statues than living men. Others were deeply interested in the ceremony of baptism.

Up to the hour of execution people were constantly arriving to witness the hanging, and the streets were densely crowded with soldiers and visitors. The sand bar in the river, the opposite bank, and all eligible places were occupied by spectators.

The Gallows

The gallows, constructed of heavy, square white oak timbers, was located on the levee opposite headquarters. It was 24 feet square, and in the form of a diamond; and about 20 feet high. The drop was held by a large rope, attached to a pole in the center of the drame, and the scaffold was supported by heavy ropes centering at this pole and attached to the one large rope running down to and fastened to the ground. The gallows was afterwards sold to John F. Meagher, who used the timbers in building a warehouse. Afterwards one of the timbers was donated to the State Historical Society and the others have been lost sign of in course of time; some having been burned in the incendiary fire of the old barn on the corner of Second and Walnut streets.

Order of Execution

We visited the prisoners in their cells an hour before the execution. Their arms were tied; some were painted and all wore blankets or shawls over their shoulders. They were seated on the floor composedly awaiting the appointed hour. They seemed cheerful, occasionally smiling and conversing together. The last hour was occupied by Father Ravoux in religious service, the prisoners following him in prayer.

Their time was thus occupied until the hour of execution.

Capt. Burt was officer of the day and officer of the guard.

The prisoners were confined in a rear room on the south side, first floor of the old Leech stone building, the windows and doors of which were securely barricaded. At an early hour in the morning admittance was denied to the public and those permitted to spend the last hour with the prisoners were the ministers, priests, reporters and officers and men of the provost guard. The irons were removed from the limbs of the prisoners, and their arms pinioned and other preparations were being made while the priests were conducting services or talking to the condemned.

While Father Ravoux was still talking to the prisoners, Capt. Redfield of the provost guard entered the prison and whispered to him that everything was in readiness, and word was communicated to Henry Millord, half-breed, who repeated it to the Indians most of whom were sitting about the floor. In a moment all were upon their feet and as the barricades were removed from the door, forming in single file, they marched quickly through the intervening room to the front door. On each side was a line of infantry, forming a pathway to the gallows,

ANTELOPE BILL 171

and as the prisoners caught sight of that instrument they hastened their steps and commenced to sing a death song. The officer of the day received them at the gallows, then following the lead of Capt. Redfield, they ascended the steps and eight men detailed to assist, placed them in position, adjusted the ropes, and placed on their heads unbleached muslin caps to hide their faces. All this time their song was continued with a dancing motion of the body.

Maj. J. R. Brown was signal officer, stationed in front of headquarters. He gave three taps upon a drum and the last was to notify Capt. W. J. Duley, stationed inside the gallows to cut the rope which held the platform. His first blow failed to do it, but a second brought down the platform with a thud, intensified by the dancing motion of the prisoners.

To those near the gallows, evidences of fear and nervousness under this trying ordeal were manifest. One Indian managed to work the noose to the back of his neck and when the drop fell he struggled terribly; others tried to clutch the blankets of those next to them; while with a spirit of defiance one went upon the gallows with a pipe in his mouth. Two clasped hands and remained in this relation till death, when their bodies were cut down. In the fall the rope of one was broken, but the fall broke his neck, and he lay quiet upon the ground until his body was taken up and hung in place. After the lapse of ten minutes one breathed but his rope was readjusted and life was soon extinct.

Drs. Seignorette of Henderson and Dr. Finch of the Seventh regiment were detailed to examine the bodies, and after hanging for half an hour they were pronounced lifeless and were cut down.

Four teams were driven to the scaffold. The bodies were deposited in the wagons and under an armed escort conveyed to the place of burial —Company K Capt. Burke, without arms, acting as a burial party. The place of burial was the low flat between front street and the river which was overgrown by swamp willows. A trench wide enough to permit the placing of two rows of bodies possibly thirty feet long, twelve wide and four to five deep, was dug in the sand on the river bank and their bodies were placed in with feet to feet, the layer was covered with coarse army blankets and over this another layer of bodies, then blankets again and the whole covered with earth.

So great was the desire for relics that crucifixes, wampum and ornaments were taken from the body before burial; others took locks of hair and a few cast off pieces of clothing. The burial escort and guard were under command of Lieut. Col. Marshall.

An Incident

Among the soldiers doing duty on this occasion was a lad of possibly 18 or 20 years, a member of Co. K, Seventh regiment. His parents and several sisters and brothers were murdered by an Indian on the gallows. The lad manifested great excitement throughout the proceedings;; his face was pale and beads of perspiration stood upon his forehead. As the drop fell he pointed a finger trembling with excitement at the prisoner and as the body dangled in the air, he gave utterance to a loud expressionless laugh which was heard and taken up by the multitude in a shout of exultations which could have been heard for a great distance.

The Resurrection

On the day of execution a number of physicians from different parts of the state as well as army surgeons, were here in person or represented by agents to procure the bodies for scientific use. During the night the grave was opened and a number of bodies taken. Others were taken on subsequent nights until the grave was almost emptied. The bodies of Cut-nose named because of a slit in one side of his nose and noted for brutality, and the Indian who broke his rope, were secured by an eminent physician of an adjoining town, thoroughly scrubbed, and were their spirits to have returned they would not have known themselves.

In the scramble for bodies, one was dropped or hidden in the timber between the grave and the town and next morning it was in the possession of a squad of soldiers. It was nude and frozen stiff and the possessors were trying to place it in position for a mark. A squad from headquarters rescued and buried it before they succeeded in their intentions, they spending the day in the guard house.

Capt. W. J. Duley, of the scouts, was the man selected to cut the rope that held the platform on which the prisoners stood. His wife had been a prisoner, taken from the Lake Shetek settlement and liberated only a few days before the execution. It is said that his first blow failed to cut the rope, because of the excitement under which he labored, but the second blow was successful and speedily sent the 38 murderers to the happy hunting grounds—if such characters there are admissable.

Camp Mystery

The Indians of the west were never so fierce and vindictive as after the close of the civil war. In the spring of 1866 there was a rush of emigrants into the new states and territories, and about this time came reports of gold and silver in several localities. The government pushed troops into new districts, established posts and the red man saw the handwriting on the wall. He realized that he would be overrun, unless the movement was checked, and the various tribes buried their differences for the time being and united all their energies on the one object of driving the white man back. The number of emigrants, land brokers, prospectors and scouts killed between May 1868 and the campaign which closed with Custer's death will never be known. It was impossible for any one to secure figures. Men were butchered singly, in pairs and in fives and tens along a frontier 1,000 miles in length, and not one case in ten was ever recorded in public print. It was the beginning of the end, and a few years ago the power of the red man was broken, and he was compelled to yield to the inevitable.

I was sent to Fort Laramie, Wyoming Territory early in the summer of 1865, having accepted the position of government scout, and I held that position all through the troubles of the next four years. It may be inferred, therefore, that I had my full share of close calls and narrow escapes. As soon as fresh troops arrived at that and other forts, and the work of subduing the Indians began in earnest, every redskin who could handle a gun was put into the field. Indeed boys not more than twelve years of age armed with bows and arrows had the opportunity to show their metal and I knew of several fights in which the young squaws took part. It was the case of do or die with the Indian and he sacrificed his pride and his legends that he might hold his own against the white soldiers. I carried dispatches between Julesburg and Laramie, and between Laramie and Fort Feltermen, and outside of this accompanied detached bodies on expeditions or scouted on my own account. There was never a day of rest and never a day when one felt sure he would live to see the sun go down. Soldiers were killed within a mile of the gates of the fort and the place was so constantly under surveillance that it was hardly possible to get in or out without being fired upon.

The strangest adventure of the whole war befell me in July 1866, and there was a mystery connected with it which has not been solved to this day. I had been out with a detached command of 160 cavalry which had scouted along the north fork of the Platte east from Laramie, to the Copper mountains. These mountains are the beginning of the Black Hills chain. On the east side of the mountains we turned to the north, rode for two days, and the cavalry then made a halt for a day and retired to Julesburg. The object was to cover as much territory as possible, and give the Indians to understand that we were aggressive. I had to report to the commander of Ft. Laramie and instead of returing and ascending the Platte I decided to try for a pass through the Copper mountains, my fellow scouts having told me that several existed. I left the cavalry camp soon after dark, it being about twenty miles east of the mountains. We had been dogged by the Indians for two days and I made my start at night to throw them off the scent. I had a jet black horse, speedy and intelligent, and the risk was not so great providing I did not run into a small band by accident.

The first two miles out of camp I walked my horse, both of us watching and listening; his senses were sharper than mine; he came to a dead halt, and pointed his nose to the west like a dog flushing a bird. That meant danger. He had been trained down fine before I got him, and was to be depended on as though he could speak. I was no sooner off his back than he lay down, and I had scarcely crouched beside him when three Indians mounted on ponies and heading to the east, passed us to the right on a walk. The nearest one was not over ten feet away, and I plainly scented the tobacco from his pipe. The ground was broken with masses of rock, outcropping here and there and it would have taken sharp eyes to detect us even at that short distance. I heard them memble and mutter as they passed on, and not until 10 minutes after the footsteps of the ponies died away in the distance did we rise and proceed. Had my horse been on the gallop, or had he been ten seconds later in discovering the redskins, I might not have got away.

Half an hour after daylight, having met with no further adventure, I was at the base of the mountains, striking the range seventeen miles from its southern end and at a place which has since been named Crook's Pass. I had little fear of finding Indians in the mountains unless it was a body passing through the gap. As soon as I was secure from the prairie I made a fire, got my coffee ready and rested two hours. Then I set out to reach the other side of the range where I would either stay by until night, or push on to Laramie, according as the signs indicated. The pass for the first half mile was fair enough for a wagon. After that it was scarcely possible for a saddle-horse to make his way. It was difficult to tell which was the main pass and which the branches, and when about half way over the mountain I came to a spot where I was completely stuck. The pass I had been following was now split into three, each one seeming to be the main pass and as there was nothing to guide me I had to take one of them at a venture. turning and ascending the Platte I decided to try

If it was not the right one I must return and take another. I went to the left and after going a few rods, found the pass or cut overgrown with bushes and badly choked up by a fall of rock. The cut was from 12 to 20 feet wide, twisting about like a creek, and gradually leading upward. The height of the bank on each side was from 50 to 200 feet, and the mountain was so densely wooded that the path was in semi-darkness.

I got my horse over the obstructions which blocked my way, and proceeded on for half a mile, without finding any great change in the general character of the pass. Then it suddenly swerved about two acres in extent to the left and debouched into a cave which nature had so walled in that the most agil Indian would have been put to his trumps to find a spot where the wall could be scaled. It would have been more in keeping with nature and the surroundings, had the cave been full of water, as small lakes of that kind are frequently found in the mountains, but it was not only solid earth, but so fertile that the sweet grass was knee high, and there were flowers without number. Before setting foot on the grass, I saw that this was the end of the pass I had followed and that I must return. I decided to let the horse graze for a while, however, and it was only after I had turned him loose that I caught sight of what appeared to be six emigrant wagons standing against the further wall. I was not sure of the character of the situation. My find seemed mysterious and I wished to run away. I should have been no more surprised to find a steamboat resting there. No emigrant had dared to penetrate so far into the Indian country in that direction and it was far away from the overland trail to California. The presence of these wagons meant a tragedy and I was loath to begin an investigation. I walked about the cave seeking to brace my courage and a few yards beyond the wagons I came upon a heap of bones which I knew to have belonged to horses or cattle. A bit farther on, a huge fire-place had been constructed of loose stones against the face of a cliff, and the smoke had blackened the wall for a distance of forty feet from the ground. There was no sign of the presence of any human being. It had been a long time since the last fire was built, as the grass was growing among the ashes and embers. The key to the mystery must be hidden in the wagons, and I returned to overhaul them. You can hardly realize the lonesome look of those vehicles. They were standing one behind the other as closely as they could be drawn and the sight of them was proof that years had gone by since they had stood there. I should say it would take at least ten years to bring about such a decay as I saw in them. They were large and heavy and made of the best material, and yet a shake would have brought any of them to the ground.

I began with the first wagon and I can easily recall the contents of each. The first wagon was piled full of harnesses or the remnants of them. Time and decay had left little, except the buckles and they were badly rusted. I should say the heap contained the harnesses of at least a dozen teams. In the second wagon were a chest, two iron kettles, a jug and a heap of mould, which probably represented clothing. I hauled the chest out and kicked it apart, but the contents had gone to mould except in the case of fifty Mexican dollars which had probably been in a buckskin bag. The third wagon also held a chest but I found nothing of value in it. I found in this wagon the rusted remains of several picks and shovels, and heaps of mould which represented either clothing or provisions. The fourth wagon was empty. The fifth contained picks and shovels and a rough wooden box. From this box I rescued a small one made of tin, and I broke that open to find $40 in state bank bills, a rude map evidently representing the Copper mountains and neighborhood and four five dollar American gold pieces.

The fifth wagon had evidently been stored with

provisions but I found nothing but mould. In the sixth were three chests, two shovels, three picks, the barrel of a rifle, a rusty ax and a keg which had held whisky. In one of the three boxes I found a silver tobacco box containing sixty dollars in Mexican gold and a note or description. It had been written on heavy paper and with good ink, but some of the words had faded entirely away and others had to be guessed. The following is the copy I made of it upon my return to Fort Laramie:

* * * there will * * * about 20 and in * * * you should take precautions * * * Have Capt. Jim see that * * * powder and lead * * * three months or more * * * same general direction * * * about due north from * * * must act for * * * shall expect * * * from man I send.

The letter was unsigned and so much of it was illegible that we could only guess at the general tenor. There had been a private expedition from Kansas years before. The party had sought shelter in the mountain valley. Had killed a portion if not all, their live stock for food. Then the men had departed but never one had returned to civilization to tell the tale. All may have been wiped out in the main pass or at the base of the mountain, or some may have died in the cave. Had the Indians ever found the wagons they would have plundered and burned them. The fact that they had not only deepened the mystery. I had notice of the discovery published far and wide in the West and on two occasions guided parties to the cave that further examination might be made, but to this day the fate of those people is a mystery.

ANTELOPE BILL'S POEM

I have travelled from the Pacific to the
    territorial lines
My trails and wanderings have been among
    the saporal and pines.

I have roughed it and endured much hard-
    ship and strife
You all may think it pleasant to hear of
    some of my life.

Here is Antelope Bill and good Texas Jack
    In good and bad weather
    Heavy loads they did pack.

Here's also our interpreter and our scouts
    three,
Who have drank many a glass and never
    had a spree,

Here's also Red Cloud and his dusky band
    We have conquered them now
    And can take them by the hand.

Cut-nose the worst of the Sioux in the lot
Of all the Indians made is the best shot.

There's also Grey Eagle who soars in the
    air,
He is not as good a warrior but still very
    fair.

Out in bleak Dakota where the buffalo
    did roam,
Where the white men are located and
    have a happy home

There is dear old Maine, the place where
    I was born
And also fair Montana upon the Big Horn

Where we once lived in shanties; they
    were made of logs of pine
Where we wiled away our young days and
    had many a merry time.

Here one evening when at supper in upon
    us came the Sioux;
Took our horses, waved their blankets and
    with shouts, bade us adieu.

We were so down-hearted then, moved our
    camp and went to bed.
At break of day we roused up, awakened
    by hells and volleys of lead.

Soup Creek Bill and Jerry Towne were
    both killed in the fight
Unknowing the Sioux conquered us then
    quickly took to flight.

ANTELOPE BILL

We left the dead boys' bodies under a
    cottonwood tree
Knowing their pleasant faces we never
    more would see.

The cactus was bad and water very stale.
But after four days more we struck Sulley's
    trail

In the distance was a cloud of dust rising
    in the west
Nearer and nearer it came and then we
    stopped to rest.

The sun was burning hot not a cloud was
    in the sky
We gave up then our lives and felt that we
    must die.

Nearer the dust cloud came at a rapid
    headlong rate
And it proved to be our friends who saved
    us from our fate.

We were taken to the camp, and kindly
    nursed and fed.
Here we told the sad story that the other
    boys were dead.

A squad was next sent out to find poor
    Towne and Bill
But the tree was never found so their bodies
    lie there still.

STRIKE-THE-REE, A ONCE FAMOUS INDIAN LATELY CALLED TO THE HAPPY HUNTING GROUNDS

Strike-The-Ree, who died a few years ago, at Yankton Agency, was a great character among the Indians and early white settlers of this territory and some very interesting anecdotes are related about him and his escapade, on the western frontier. A gentleman who has had a large experience as a hunter and trapper, during the early days of the territory, relates the following anecdote which he obtained from "Old Dakota," an old French trapper in 1865. Old Dakota was then about fifty years of age, a Canadian Frenchman and had lived all his life on the frontier with the Indians. For several years prior to 1843 Old Dakota had roamed the wild western prairies. He had hunted with the Shoshones of the Pacific coast. He had been chased by the Crows and Blackfeet near the head waters of the Yellow Stone, and had held high carnival in the "bull pens" of Mexico. He had worked for the American Fur Company and had ranged all through the Black Hills, Wind River and Big Horn mountains as a trapper and Indian trader.

Among the Indians who located around Fort Rice when the tribe paid their visit to trade with the white men was a young and buxom Indian girl, who after one or two interviews took forcible possession of the young Frenchman's heart. Nothing was more common and according to the custom than he should marry this fair child of the prairies. But alas! the young squaw's father refused to part with the girl unless the Frenchman gave him a good horse in exchange. Unfortunately the young trapper had parted with all his hard year's earnings ere his heart was taken by storm. The Frenchman was "broke." He had not the wherewith to buy a horse and without a horse he could not secure the dusky maiden for his wife. The trapping season was long since over, and it lacked a month of the time for starting on the fall expedition. However the young trapper shoul-

ANTELOPE BILL

dered his gun and left the comforts and amusements of Ft. Rice to seek the haunts of the wild game hoping to raise by the prosecution of the chase, the means of winning the Indian girl from her relatives. In the pursuit of game, in due time, he appeared at the Cannon Ball river with a goodly supply of furs. Two months had passed in trapping, when, following a new path, the adventurous trapper entered a deep and woody glen. Pushing his way through he at length came out on the edge of an open glade near the mouth of the river, where he discovered a "mystic" lodge of the Yankton Indians. Under a peculiar custom of this tribe of the Sioux Indians, no young brave, though his father might have been the bravest of the tribe could rank himself among the warriors and be entitled to marry, or to enjoy the many other rights of citizenship until he had performed some act of daring and intrepidity. In the early spring therefore, the young men of proper age, banded themselves together in small companies and took to the woods—like knight errants of old —in search of adventure and peril. Having found a retired spot, they formed a huge conical-shaped hut, constructed of p o l e s and branches of trees of from twenty to thirty feet high lashed together at the top with strips of rawhide. Buffalo, beads, furs, kettles, scalps and other offerings, were hung up inside of this rude temple, as offerings to the great spirit and after many days of feasting, dancing, and mystic rites, the hut was abandoned, the vow taken and the band started on their campaign. Death was the sure portion of him who should be known to enter and desecrate it during their absence.

Upon one of these mystic lodges the young Frenchman had sumbled. Within the lodge were articles of more than sufficient value to purchase the necessary horse, yet, in spite of the temptation, the young trapper had too much honor to rob the Indian temple, and was about to move away when a hand was laid on his shoulder and a young brave stepped out from behind him and said:

"My white brother has the eyes of a lynx, and the cunning of a fox. He starts out on his journey early in the season."

The hunter laughed as he replied:

"My wigwam is empty, and I would make it warm for the sister of the great chief. What luck!"

The young brave shook his head gravely as he pointed to his empty belt and said:

"Five moons have passed and gone since we left our homes many miles down the river, and our hatchet has not yet been raised. The Arickarees are cowards and hide in their wigwams."

In a little valley, surrounded by cottonwood trees, and willows on the level prairie, the Indian camp was pitched. Though the silence of the place was unbroken, twelve young Indians were congregated around a fire, partaking of their evening meal. The trapper was cordially received by them and especially so by "Young Strike," as the hunter had given him the previous season the handsomest tomahawk pipe in the tribe.

"Old Dakota" stayed the greater part of two days with the Yankton Indian war party, and started back in the direction of the Missouri river, hoping that he would meet with a good market in selling his furs, and thus be enabled to gain the hand of his sweetheart. But alas! When he reached his journey's end, after many days of weary travel, he learned that his faithless lady love, had, during his absence. married a French Creole, and that they had taken their departure.

The Indian maiden had been flattered by the newcomer, who dressed in a new suit of buckskin and mounted on a high spirited running horse. And her avaricious papa was easily persuaded by the wily Creole—who had recently deserted a Mandan squaw and a troop of piebald children in the upper country—to accept of his running horse and five buffalo robes for the privilege of becoming his father-in-law. Wishing to avoid the just vengeance that would be meted out to them by the young trapper on his return, they had skipped for more congenial parts. The young Frenchman was deeply affected and disappointed at the turn his romance of love had taken, and it took many weeks of dissipation ere he could obliterate from his mind's eye, the image of the fair young girl. After squandering the proceeds of his winter's work, he purchased a new trapping outfit and went toward the setting sun a sadder but wiser man. During this campaign he was joined by Young-Strike-The Ree, and together they hunted through the country now known as the Black Hills and it was then they first discovered that gold existed there. Strike-The-Ree has since stated that the Indians found little lumps of gold which they used for ornaments. He says that the white traders (the American Fur Company), traded beads and blankets for these lumps of gold.

After this campaign "Old Dakota" went west and hunted through California and Mexico, and did not again strike the Ree till after the great Sioux Indian massacre in 1862, when "Strike" narrated the events as they occurred then. He said that he was forced into the war upon the whites, through a combination of circumstances and that he was instrumental in saving many whites from the savages, who attacked the settlers under Rain-in-the-face, Hole-in-the-day, Little Heart and others. In 1864 Strike-The-Ree was a familiar character upon the streets of Yankton, and while there were scarcely 25 in the village, "Old Strike" was unanimously elected mayor. This was considered quite a joke at the time. "Strike the Ree" was a conspicuous figure during the Indian massacre of 1862, and nothing pleased him more than to recount his adventures during that memorable event, when he claimed to have saved many of the white settlers from a torturing death, by assisting them to escape to a place of safety. In one instance he says he carried a baby two miles, and assisted the sick mother to reach soldiers who were at that time somewhere on the Minnesota river. The old Indian was called to the happy hunting grounds at the age of 102 years.

In conclusion I will say that the horrid details of the Indian atrocities we have endeavored to avoid and hope that the young man who reads this, if dissatisfied with his surroundings may learn to be content.

"THE AUTHOR."

ITEMS ABOUT MARSHALL, MINN.

Marshall is the county seat of Lyon county, and centrally located, one of the most enterprising towns in the state, one of handsome residences, magnificent brick blocks, and a wealth of beautiful shade trees; has about 2,500 population, two railroads, C. and N. W., and G. N.; has a large roller flouring mill, electric plant and city water works, supplied by an artesian well 400 feet deep throwing an abundance of water at over sixty pounds, pressure three of these wells being in the village. Marshall is surrounded by a rich agricultural country and has all church and school facilities, the high school being in the first grade. All business is represented. Home seekers can find here everything socially and otherwise, to make life pleasant.

Marshall has much reason to boast of its town; people courteous and hospitable to strangers, honorable and upright in their dealings, and take high rank as good citizens.

The U. S. and R. R. Land offices are located here.

All communications will be answered freely by addressing

BEACH & JOHNSON,
Marshall, Minn.

Lyon County, Minn.

With a view of making better known the many superior advantages possessed by Southwestern Minnesota in general, and Lyon county in particular, over other more widely known localities, and to encourage good practical farmers to locate here, believe that there is a large class of farmers who have not the means to purchase high priced lands and yet are backward in going where land is cheap, and being obliged to face the hardships and privations incident to a new country, but who would be glad to change their location where they could enjoy all the advantages of an old settled country, and still be able to buy cheap land. The writer's object therefore is to advertise this county. Not with the intention of booming it, not with the desire of painting a pretty word picture that would be dispelled under the clear, penetrating gaze of cautions land buyer, but for the purpose of making a clear plain, straightforward statement of facts as they exist, and which will bear the closest scrutiny. In fact, we want investigation. This is as good a country as the sun ever shown upon and it should be known. To those people then, who are seeking a change of location for the purpose of bettering their condition. the writer commands a careful investigation.

Lyon county has low taxes, good roads, cheap lands, cheap lumber, first class schools, a productive soil, an exceedingly healthy climate, prosperous farmers and business men, all different church denominations, all the leading secret society organizations, land at 15 dollars an acre, some higher and some lower. Standing invitations to good practical farmers.

The fact that the state experimental farm is located in Lyon county, is quite a drawing card for the county. Farmers are able to get a good many pointers from the result obtained on the farm.

The star of empire seems to be taking its way to Lyon County, Minn.

There are over ninety miles of railroad in Lyon County.

There is always an opening for good farmers.

There are thirty-five grain elevators in the county.

The author of this book has lived in the county 31 years.

Index

Acton, 122, 123
Adams, Frank, 81
A-e-cha-ga, 161
Agency, 31, 50
Agency, Lower, 9, 10, 30, 32, 34, 35, 50, 59, 122, 132-134, 140, 152, 156
Agency, Upper, 10, 12, 30, 49, 52, 120, 122, 165
Agency, Yellow Medicine, 11, 54
Akipa, 166
Am-da-cha, 156
American flag, 12
American Fur Co., 188, 192
Anderson, Capt., 132
Anderson, Mary, 162
Ange, Hypolite, 160
Anson, John, 87, 88
Apple Creek, 101
Arickarees, 190
Arnold, Adjt., 150

Bailey, Capt., 117
Baker family, 122
Balland, Joe, 123
Beach & Johnson, 194
Beaver Creek, 31, 124, 132, 135, 158, 162
Beaver Falls, 96
Belgian muskets, 117
Belle Plain, 118, 130
Benton, Fort, 71, 81, 84
Big Cottonwood, 153
Big Horn, 184, 188
Big Stone Lake, 96
Big Woods, 121, 133, 162
Birch Coolie, 10, 115, 132, 136, 137, 152, 158
Bishop, Sergeant, 60
Bismarck, 101

Black Foots, (Blackfeet), 89, 188
Black Hills, 176, 188, 192
Bloods, 71, 89
Blue Earth, 93, 147
Boardman, J. D., 35
Boston, 73, 80
Brown Family, 83, 157
Brown, Major Joe R., 41, 50, 132-145, 137, 151, 165, 171
Brusson, 123
Buck, Mr., 90
Burbank, 104
Burke, Capt., 172
Burt, Capt., 170

Calhoun, 64
California, 180, 192
Campbell, Baptiste, 93, 157-160
Campbell, Joseph, 159
Campbell, Scott, 158
Canadian Northwest, 102
Canfil, Oscar, 35
Cannon Ball river, 189
Carver, 118
Catholic, 103, 150, 168
Cedar City, 45
Chan-ka-hda, 162
Chas-kay-dan, 157
Chay-tan-hoon-ka, 162
Chippewa, 19, 28, 46, 95, 119, 145, 161
"Chris", 47
Christ, 111, 154, 163
Christian, 120, 165
Colt, 87
Company A, 6th Regiment, 117, 118
Company B, Fifth Regiment, 57, 68-70

Company B, 6th Regiment, 117
Company C, Fifth Minn., 54, 59, 69, 70
Company C, 6th Regiment, 117
Company F, 6th Regiment, 12, 117, 131, 142
Company K, Seventh Regiment, 172, 173
Cook, Jim, 86
Copper mountains, 176, 177, 181
Cottonwood River, 83, 126
Cow Island, Montana, 81, 84, 85, 87
Crawford, Charles, 34, 35
Crees, 102
Cromsie, Edward, 34
Crooks, Col., 67, 129
Crook's Pass, 178
Crow Indians, 82, 84, 123, 188
Cullen guard, 129, 132
Cullen, W. J., 129
Culver, Lieut. Norman K., 69
Custer, 67, 175
Cut Nose, 22, 157, 173

Dacotah, 164, 165
Dakota, 128, 150, 157, 184
Daly, Miss Mary, 34
Densmore, Ben, 142
Devils Lake, 103
Dodd, Capt., 44
Donnelly, Lieut. Gov., 130
Do-wan-sa, 155
Duly, Capt. W. J., 171, 174

Eschelle, Henry, 34

Estlick, Mr., 129
E-tag-doo-ta, 156
Europe, 95

"Father Abraham", 115
Father Andrew, 103, 104
"Favorite, The", 8
Feltermen, Fort, 176
Fifth regiment, 67, 69, 124
Finch, Dr., 172
First Minnesota, 33, 80
Flandreau, Judge, 126, 128
Forbes', 123, 124, 156
Forest City, 121, 129
Forsyth, 64, 67
Four Mile Lake, 139
French Creole, 191
Frenchman, 41, 75, 161, 188, 190, 192

Galbraith, Mrs., 36
Garvie, Mr. Stewart B., 37, 40, 45, 47, 159, 160
Gere, Lt. Thomas P., 54, 55, 59, 62, 68-70
German, Mr., 34
Germans, 31, 42, 85-87, 126, 154
Given, Mr. Nelson, 18, 25, 34
Gleason, George, 35, 49, 50, 140, 158
Glencoe, 56, 118, 131
God, 20, 37, 65, 136, 150, 154, 163, 165
Goodell, Mr., 13-19, 22, 23, 32, 39, 40, 43, 44, 46
Goodell, Mrs., 16, 19, 23, 32
Gorman, Lieut. James, 57, 69

Grant, Capt., 117, 118, 132, 134, 135, 142
Gray Bird, 133
Great Spirit, 19, 21, 66, 160, 164, 166
Grey Eagle, 22, 184

Hall, Capt. Francis, 54
Hamharn, Mrs., 34
Hamline University, 12, 115
Ha-pan, 155
Hawkins, T., 35
Hayes, Mary, 19, 32
Hay-pe-dan, 156
Hay-pin-kpa, 159
Hda-hin-day, 162
Helena, 71, 72
Hendricks, Capt. Mark, 136
Henry (brother), 8, 14, 18, 52, 143
Higgins, Amos W., 159
Higgins, Mrs. Josephine, 159
Hill, Mr., 35, 40
Hindman, Rev. Mr., 124
Hin-han-shoon-ko-yag-ma-ne, 152
Hole-in-the-day, 193
Howitzer, 28, 29, 54, 55, 59, 136, 137
Hubbard, Gen. Lucius F., 67, 68
Huggins, Mr. Amos, 129
Hurd, Mrs., 129
Hutchinson, 157, 159, 161

Inkpaduta, 55
Iowa, 128, 129
Iron Blower, 153
Irvine, William, 138

Jackson, 67

Jewett Family, 92-94
Jones family, 122
Jones, Ordinance-Sergeant John, 57, 59, 63, 64, 69, 136
Josh, 29
Julesburg, 176

Kansas, 182
Kennedy, 31, 34
Kimball, Capt., 81, 82
Ko tan-in-koo, 162

La Batte, 123, 147
La Belle, 40
Lac-qui Parle, 15, 129, 143 159
Laramie, Fort, 175-178, 182
Leavenworth, 82
Le Claire, Baptiste, 98
Leech, 151, 170
Le Sueur, 93
Lincoln, Camp, 148
Lincoln, President, 147, 150
Little Crow, Chief, 11, 31, 53, 57-62, 64, 65, 68, 80, 101-103, 122, 125, 126, 127, 133, 145, 153, 154, 157-160
Little Heart, 193
Lone Tree Lake, 140
Lynde, James, 123
Lyon County, 94, 194-196

Ma-hoo-way-ma, 162
Mah-pe-o-ke-ne-jin, 157
Maine, 7, 184
Ma-ka-ta-e-na-jin, 161
Makpeyahwetah, Chief, 121
"Man-Who-Closed-the-Gate", 53

Mandan, 191
Manderfield, Anthony, 97
Manitoba, 102
Manitou, 19
Mankato, Minnesota, 7, 16, 47, 52, 83, 92-94, 96, 128, 130, 133, 147-149
March, Mrs. Jane H., 34
Marsh, Capt. John F., 28, 56, 69, 124, 152, 155, 157
Marshall, Lieut. Col., 131, 142, 147, 172
Marshall, Minnesota, 194
Ma-ya-bon-doo, 152
Ma-za-boom-doo, 153
McClellan, 116
McGrew, Sergeant James G., 58, 59, 62, 63, 69
McLaren, Maj., 136
McLean, Corporal, 56
McPhail, Col. Samuel, 129, 136
M'dewakantons, 122
Meagher, John F., 169
Merriam, Capt., 117
Mexican, 181, 182, 192
Milk river, 84
Miller, Col., 149-151
Miller, N. A., 34
Millord, Henry, 150, 157, 170
Minneapolis, 67, 94, 95, 105
Minnesota, 12, 53, 68, 69, 75, 80, 95, 105, 106, 115, 116, 128, 129, 141
Minnesota river, 7, 13, 18, 40, 53, 68, 116, 117, 147, 148, 152, 156, 158, 160, 193
Mississippi, 20, 81

Missouri river, 20, 81, 84, 85, 87, 101-103, 191
Montana, 87, 184
Montevideo, 145
Mouse river, 104
Muller, Dr. Alfred, 70
Murfreesborough, Tenn., 141
Murphy, Frank, 72
Myrick, 123

Na-pa-shue, 160
New Auburn, 56
New Ulm, 44, 52, 53, 57, 58, 83, 96, 97, 104, 119, 124-130, 133, 148, 152, 153, 155, 160, 161
Northrup, Capt. Anson, 67

"Old Dakota", 187, 188, 191, 192
Other Day, John, 32, 34, 35, 37, 40, 41, 44, 46, 125
Other Day, Mrs. John, 34, 41, 46, 47
O-va-tay-ta-wa, 155
Oxford, Miss., 70
O-ya-tag-a-kso, 162

Pacific, 183, 188
Patrol, Frederic, 34
Patrolle, Pete, 32, 33
Patterson's Rapids, 135
Patwell, 152, 153, 155, 162
Pa-za-koo-tag-ma-ne, 161
Pembina, 104
Pettibone, Hermen, 142
Platte, 176-178
Potomac, 116
Protestant, 150, 154
Ptan-doo-ta, 152

Qua-ma-ne, 154
Quinn, Peter, 69, 155

Rain-in-the-face, 193
Ramsey, Gov., 119
Randall, Hon. Benjamin H., 62, 69
Rattling Runner, 154
Ravoux, Fr. A., 165, 169, 170
Rda-in-you-ka, 154, 164
Red Cloud, 22, 183
Red Face, 156
Redfield, Capt., 170, 171
Red Iron, Chief, 119, 159, 166
Red Leaf, 153
Red Legs, 123
Red Otter, 152
Red river, 92
Red Wing, Minnesota, 12, 115, 116, 142
Redwood, 11, 116, 119, 139, 147, 158
Redwood Falls, 75
Redwood Ferry, 69
Release, Camp, 36, 80, 124, 145, 146, 154
Renville, Charley, 27, 40, 41, 73, 75-80
Renville County, 96
Renville, Joseph, 154
Renville Rangers, 30, 53, 69, 143
Reynolds, Joe, 11
Rice Creek, 122, 161
Rice, Fort, 188, 189
Richardson, Mr., 131
Ridgley, Fort, 10, 28, 30, 34, 41, 53-57, 67-69, 116, 119, 124-128, 130-132, 136, 138, 139, 152, 155-157, 162
Riggs, Rev. Mr. S. R., 125, 150, 165
Ripley, Fort, 54, 56, 68
River Bottom, 53
"Roberts(Jeanette", 8
Roberts, Louis, 98, 113, 114, 123
Rock, Little, 75-80
Roman Nose, 64
Round Wind, 154

Sacred Heart Creek, 124
St. Cloud, 104
St. Joseph, 104
St. Paul, 35, 46, 49, 53, 95, 102, 104, 113, 114
St. Peter, 47, 57, 118, 126, 129, 130, 133
Sawyer, Charles, 34
Sawyer, Misses Mary & Lizzie, 34
Schurch, John, 94-104, 106
Seignorette, Dr., 172
Seventh regiment, 131, 142, 147, 172, 173
Seventh Minnesota, 116
Shakopee, 46, 117, 118, 122
Sheehan, Timothy J., 28, 29, 53-57, 59, 62, 65-70, 127, 136
Shetek, Lake, 129, 174
Shoon-ka-ska, 155
Shoshones, 188
Sibley, Gen. H. H., 36, 53, 80, 117, 118, 124, 129, 130, 133, 134, 135, 147, 157, 164
Singer, The, 155
Sinks, Noah, 18, 29, 34, 44
Sioux, 8, 9, 11, 19, 23, 27,

28, 36, 49, 50, 53, 54, 68, 73, 75, 80, 82-84, 89, 94, 95, 98, 100, 102-106, 108, 112, 183, 184, 189, 192
Sisseton Sioux, 98, 99, 103, 120
Sixth Regiment, 12, 115, 117, 129, 132, 142, 146, 147
Snelling, Fort, 116, 146, 147, 158
Soldier's Lodge, 158
Soup Creek Bill, 184, 185
Spencer, George, 124
Spirit Lake, 129
Springfield, 87
Standing Buffalo, 26, 98-102
State Historical Society, 169
State Normal School, 94
Stevens, Mr., 93
Strike-The-Ree, 187, 191-193
Strout, Capt., 159
Sulley's trail, 185
Sun river, 71, 73, 89
Swan Lake, 155
Swan, Mary, 153
Swedes, 42

Ta-joo, 152
Ta-ta-hde-dan, 161
Ta-ta-ka-kay, 159
Ta-tah-me-ma, 154
Ta-ti-mi-ma, 166
Tatonka Naji, 98
Ta-zoo, 166, 167
Te-he-do-ne-cha, 152
Texas Jack, 183
Third Minn. regiment, 140, 141
Tinkling Walker, 154

Toon-kan-e-chan-tag-ma-ne, 156
Toon kan-ko-yag-e-na-jin, 161
Towne, Jerry, 184, 185
Trescott, Sergeant, 56

United States, 53, 68, 69, 103, 146, 158

Van Raveaux, Rev., 165, 169, 170
Virginia, 116

Wabasha, 123, 156, 164
Waconta, 123
Wa-he-hua, 153
Wahpetons, 120
Wa-kan-tau-ka, 160
Wakefield, Dr. J. L., 18, 29, 35, 44, 45, 49
Wakefield, Mrs., 35, 49-52, 158
Walker, Sacret, 159
Wa-pa-doo-ta, 153
Warner, Mrs. Eleanor, 34
Wa-she-choon, 161
Washington, 41, 149, 165
Wayne, 67
Webster, 64
Webster family, 122
Welch, 140-142
West St. Paul, 138
Whipple, J. C., 58, 59, 62, 70
Whitcomb, Mr., 121
White Dog, 155
Williams, Miss Mattie, 152, 153
Williamson, Rev. Dr., 27, 125, 154, 165

Williston, Capt., 116
Wilson, Miss Clara D., 122
Wilson, Prof. H. B. (Capt.), 12, 115, 117
Wind Maker, 159
Wind River, 188
Winnebago, 19, 83
Wood Lake, 12, 53, 115, 140, 141, 143, 152, 154, 160, 162
Wy-a-tah-ta-wa, 152

Wyckoff, Clerk, 57
Wyoming Territory, 175

Yankton, 101, 103, 187, 189, 191, 193
Yellow Medicine, 10, 13, 18, 32, 52, 54, 55, 80, 124, 125, 133, 134, 139, 140, 142, 146, 147, 160
Yellow Stone, 188
Young, Antoin, 123

*This book was designed by Harlow Ross
and set in 12 point Benedictine
on a 14 point base. It has been printed by
the craftsmen at Meyers Printing Company
on Warren's "Old Style" laid finish paper.*

*It is issued in an edition limited
to 550 copies of which
this is number . . .*

34